TRANSFORMING LITERACY TEACHING
IN THE ERA OF HIGHER STANDARDS

Model Lessons and Practical Strategies That Show You
How to Integrate the Standards to Plan and Teach With Confidence

Karen Biggs-Tucker and Brian Tucker

■ SCHOLASTIC

New York • Toronto • London • Auckland • Sydney
Mexico City • New Delhi • Hong Kong • Buenos Aires

DEDICATION

To my husband Brian, and my son Jason, who have and continue to help me transform myself for the better each and every day. You're the best! —*K.B.T.*

To my wife Karen, and every educator who has had a hand in transforming me as a literacy teacher. —*B.T.*

ACKNOWLEDGMENTS

Many of the ideas in this book were influenced by the collaborative conversations we've had with our colleagues and the motivation to keep writing was given to us by the people in our lives who are always there when needed them. Many thanks to . . .

- Maria Walther, our mentor, inspiration and the best "writing pal" ever! Thanks for believing in us and helping us make this dream come true!

- Donna Clavelli and the staff at Wild Rose Elementary School who has given us the "roots and wings" to grow as literacy learners and teachers. "Super teachers, super kids, that is just the way it is!"

- Our Judson MLIT and DLIT colleagues who remind us that lifelong learning is more that just words on a page, and to Dr. Steven Layne, who has always looked to move us beyond the "walls of our classrooms" and out into the world.

- Our fifth graders at Wild Rose Elementary School whose love of learning has helped get us out of bed every morning and look forward to walking into the classroom to learn beside you each and every day. Thanks for being such great readers, writers, and thinkers!

- Joanna Davis-Swing, our editor. Thanks for the extra hours you put in with the "newbies" on this project. Your patience, your belief in us, and you never-ending ability to make the book better with each and every revision! Thanks for taking this journey with us!

❄   ❄   ❄

Cover Designer: Jorge J. Namerow
Editor: Joanna Davis-Swing
Interior Designer: Sarah Morrow
Copyright © 2015 by Karen Biggs-Tucker and Brian Tucker
All rights reserved. Published by Scholastic Inc.
Printed in the U.S.A.
ISBN: 978-0-545-65335-0

1 2 3 4 5 6 7 8 9 10   40   22 21 20 19 18 17 16 15

Contents

A Call to Action

We are excited to share with you the new essentials for teaching literacy in the era of higher standards. We view the implementation of higher standards as a call to action to all teachers, but especially those of us in the intermediate grades, to create effective and meaningful instruction for our students. These new standards combine many of the objectives that have cluttered our plan books for years and streamline them into fewer, clearer goals for our students. They also raise the bar for our learners in terms of the critical thinking that they are expected to do, not only in our classrooms but also in the world that they will enter when they leave school. The world in which we live and teach is constantly changing, and we need to be brave enough to change with it. The standards themselves can provide the guidance for us to transform our teaching to lead our students to become the 21st-century lifelong learners that our society demands them to be.

As teachers of students in the intermediate grades, we also know that the standards will be followed by an assessment, and we try to prepare our students for the assessment that looms on the horizon. But, like you, we struggle to balance our efforts at preparing students for "The TEST" with instilling in them a lifelong love of learning. Is there a way to accomplish both of these goals without driving ourselves crazy in the process? Our answer is yes! Over the last several years, we have worked to gather the resources to do just that, with the literature, authentic learning experiences, and best practices that we have found to be tried and true, not only in the research but also in our day-to-day interactions with students.

In this book, we'll show you how to plan literacy instruction that will be both meaningful and manageable for your students and will transform your practice. To help guide you, the book is divided into two parts. Part 1 consists of four chapters. In the first chapter, you will see how the standards are just one more bend in the road on your journey to grow as a reading and writing educator. We'll share tips for creating a classroom environment where your learners will develop the skills outlined in the standards documents and we'll get you started. In the next chapter, we will show you how to integrate literacy with the content areas and balance instruction throughout your day. In the third and fourth chapters, we'll share our thinking about how reading and writing workshops enhance the implementation of the standards in your literacy instruction. Part 2 includes three chapters that guide you in transforming teaching routines, like book talks and creating anchor charts, that are already part of your daily literacy instruction. Our goal is to show you how to create rich inquiry experiences out of your current routines. Luckily, this isn't hard to do. We've included many scenarios and show how you can make minor teaching moves that will nudge your children toward reaching the complexity of thought and application of knowledge that the standards expect. As an added bonus, this type of planning also saves instructional time, something we all strive for! Finally, in the online resources (see page 160), you will find planning guides to support you in the complex task of mapping out literacy instruction. Page 6 provides a chart that details how the ideas in this book will help you transform your literacy teaching.

You'll notice we've used the Common Core State Standards (CCSS) as exemplar standards to guide our thinking. We realize that there is much debate across the nation about the standards and certainly about the assessments that accompany them. Whether you are teaching in a state that has adopted the Common Core State Standards or one in which you are developing your own standards that reflect the rigor found in the CCSS, we think we can all agree that readjusting our expectations to ensure that learners are successful long after they leave our classroom is an valuable, ongoing educational conversation.

TRANSFORMING TEACHING	
I have too many separate skills and strategies to teach—where do I begin? How do I fit it all in across the school year?	We will show you how to integrate learning experiences to help students understand the connections among foundational skills, language skills, reading, writing, thinking, listening, and speaking. In addition, the online resources (see page 160) contain guides that will help you as you begin to plan units on your own throughout the school year!
I'm always running out of time and feeling rushed during my reading and writing workshops. How do I make more time for my learners to read, converse, and write?	You'll learn how to save time and teach with more depth by selecting standards-focused learning targets or "big ideas" to explore in both reading and writing workshops at the same time, or during a combined literacy workshop.
How do I make sure that my students meet the rigor of the standards, but also have authentic learning experiences?	This book offers experiences that will help your students meet the standards through standards-based learning experiences related to them, but also through experiences that are authentic and, dare we say, engaging!
I'm looking for the best books to read aloud to my students to spark collaborative conversations about texts, to serve as mentor texts for writing, and to assist me in teaching the concepts found in the language standards. Can you recommend some titles?	Both of us are children's literature fanatics. Most of the standards-focused learning experiences in this book will begin with a recently published or "old favorite" book suggestion or two . . . or more!

Transforming Teaching

You'll notice the Transforming Teaching charts just like the one above throughout this book. Why? Because, in our evolution as literacy teachers, we are continually examining our current practice to reflect on how our teaching choices impact student learning. Then, we synthesize new learning from professional development experiences with our growing knowledge of our students to refine our craft or take it to the "next" step. So, whether you are using the Common Core State Standards or not, our hope is that this book helps you examine your practice, then nudges you to ponder and converse with colleagues to determine how you can transform your teaching and students' learning experiences.

Let's begin our work together as we transform our teaching!

 Transforming Literacy Teaching in the Era of Higher Standards, Grades 3–5 © 2015 by Karen Biggs-Tucker and Brian Tucker, Scholastic Teaching Resources

Chapter I

Going on a Journey

Making the Move

We begin and end the year by reading Patricia MacLachlan's *What You Know First* with our students. (If you don't know this title, it will be our first official book recommendation!) It is a beautiful story about a young child who is leaving home and mourning the loss of the old, familiar things. Mother tells her that even though she is going into a new place, she will bring much of what she knows with her. We love to use this book to let our students know that they, too, bring many of their own experiences with them to school, which make the transition to the new less scary. We assure them that the background knowledge they bring prepares them for the learning that awaits them, not only in our classrooms but in their lives beyond school walls.

As we thought about writing this book, we reflected on our own journey into the era of curricular standards and recalled how, initially, we considered it unfamiliar territory. But as we began to make the connections to our original best practices, we saw how we could transform those practices into new teaching that would support our students as they encounter the new standards. We realized that this journey would be a powerful experience both for our students and for us. We hope that as you begin to reflect and think about "what you know first," what is in your classrooms, and what is in the standards—you will see that you can make this journey, too!

Go online to view a classroom video tour. See page 160 for details.

A Yearlong Journey

One of the biggest shifts in our thinking about the standards was that they represent end-of-the-year goals for our students. The CCSS present a portrait of a learner at the end of the year. This thinking may be unfamiliar for many of us because we are used to having benchmarks showing us where our students should be at particular times throughout the year. Each of our journeys toward those end-of-year goals will be a bit different because the needs of our individual students are unique. How, then, do we effectively implement the standards-based instruction for *all* of our diverse learners? Every day, we must ask ourselves what it is that we want our students to know and be able to do. The answers to these questions are found within the standards document itself. The standards have given us the end goal, and it's up to us to create the road map to get our students there. In the pages that follow, we'll peek into our classrooms to show you how we create an environment that nurtures our learners throughout the year, guiding and supporting them as they stride toward the ambitious goals laid out in the standards—starting on the very first day of school!

Build a classroom atmosphere where children become self-reliant, independent learners.

A Portrait of a Learner Who Meets the Rigorous Standards

❋ Becomes a self-directed, independent learner.

❋ Builds strong content-area knowledge.

❋ Adjusts communication based on audience, task, purpose, and discipline.

❋ Comes to understand other perspectives and cultures.

❋ Comprehends as well as critiques.

❋ Values evidence.

❋ Uses technology and digital media strategically and capably.

Common Core State Standards (CCSS) for English Language Arts *(NGA Center and CCSSO, 2010, p. 7)*

Create a Classroom Environment That Encourages Self-Directed, Independent Learning

Our classroom environment reflects what we value most—to ourselves, to our stakeholders, and most of all, to our students! We strive to make sure that everything we say, do, and exhibit in our classroom builds a community of learners, each of whom is empowered to become an individual the CCSS standards define as "self-directed and independent." We recognize that community building begins on Day 1 and continues until the last day of school. We also know that our community grows out of the work of teachers in the grades below us, and we are providing the building blocks of learning for the grades that follow. But what does that classroom environment look and sound like? We'll give you some of the strategies that have worked for us and for our students as we have strived to develop self-directed, independent learning within and beyond our classrooms.

WHAT WE SAY AND HOW WE SAY IT

Recognizing the importance of language in the classroom is one important building block for creating independent learners. When teachers employ carefully thought-out language, it creates a model for students' interactions and helps students internalize language patterns for those interactions. That thinking helps lead them toward the essential recognition of themselves as independent learners. One way we do this is by modeling our thinking and then encouraging students to go back and try it on their own. When we say, "I wonder what the

Transforming Literacy Teaching in the Era of Higher Standards, Grades 3–5 © 2015 by Karen Biggs-Tucker and Brian Tucker, Scholastic Teaching Resources

author wanted the reader to think after reading that page in the book. Let's go back and see what clues he gave us and figure it out together," we are modeling the way we want them to think when reading independently.

One literacy mentor who has guided our thinking regarding the way we talk in the classroom is Peter Johnston. His book *Choice Words: How Language Affects Children's Learning* (2004) prompted us to begin to model language that would help our students start to think of themselves as independent thinkers and learners. Ellin Oliver Keene is another literacy mentor who has taught us the importance of becoming the language role models in our classrooms. By doing this, we help our students learn the language of learning and grow into the intellectual life around them (Vygotsky, 1962). If you have not had the opportunity to learn from some of these literacy leaders, we encourage you to sample some of the titles listed in the box at right. Below we've summarized some of the thinking that we gained from Johnston's book that we now incorporate into our classroom environment.

Create opportunities where children learn how to be respectful listeners.

Professional Books About Using Language to Enhance Learning Experiences

* ❋ *Choice Words: How Our Language Affects Children's Learning* (Johnston, 2004)

* ❋ *Comprehension Through Conversation: The Power of Purposeful Talk in the Reading Workshop* (Nichols, 2006)

* ❋ *Opening Minds: Using Language to Change Lives* (Johnston, 2012)

* ❋ *Talk About Understanding: Rethinking Classroom Talk to Enhance Comprehension* (Keene, 2012)

Develop students' respect for themselves and for one another. Creating an atmosphere of mutual respect among students is an important building block for any classroom, and it all depends on what we say and how we say it.

Here are some simple ways to foster a respectful atmosphere early in the school year:

* be interested in what every student says
* listen to what every child says and encourage classmates to do the same
* make eye contact with each student when he or she is speaking
* value student opinions about a variety of topics throughout the school day

(Johnston, 2004); (Allington & Johnston, 2002)

Focus on comments that honor process vs. product. Students feel more confident when approaching a task they believe they can accomplish. Focus your feedback on the steps along the way that lead students to the learning rather than the end product. Telling a student "This strategy seems to be working well for you," or "You're really on the right track with your thinking," helps them to focus on the strategy that they are employing in their work rather than the work itself. It also helps us understand how students are thinking, so we can better guide their process. Of course, guiding their thinking ultimately helps them attain the end goal. In focusing on the process, we help struggling learners persist by giving them constructive feedback that will keep them motivated and provide them the information that they need in order to progress in the learning process.

Keep in mind that, "The purpose of feedback is to improve conceptual understanding or increase strategic options while developing stamina, resilience, and motivation—expanding the vision of what is possible and how to get there. Perhaps we should call it *feedforward* rather than feedback" (Johnston, 2012, p. 48).

Think about learners on a continuum of experience rather than in terms of "good" and "bad." For years, we created charts at the beginning of the year entitled "What Do Good Readers Do?" and

"What Do Good Writers Do?" We never realized that these charts communicated to our students that if there were "good" readers and "good" writers, there must also be "bad" readers and "bad" writers in our classrooms. Certainly, this is a message that we never meant to communicate! Now our charts say, "What Do Experienced Readers Do?" and "What Do Experienced Writers Do?" This small change in our language communicates a much more accurate message to our learners. We are all more experienced learners today than we were last year, or even last week!

Like changing any habit, changing your actions and reactions will take time and practice, especially if you've been doing something in your classroom practice for a long time. Be patient with yourself as you are learning a new skill— just as you would be with your students if they were mastering a new learning strategy. We find it useful to have a few helpful phrases or questions nearby to remind us what deliberate, conscious actions sound like in our classrooms. We also know that making conscious choices in how our environment looks helps create a productive classroom community.

Asking/Answering One Another in a Self-Directed, Independent Thinking Classroom

❋ What did anyone notice?

❋ Let's see if I've got this right . . .

❋ Can anyone add to his or her thinking?

❋ Would you agree with that? Why/why not?

❋ Do you have the same thinking, or is your thinking different? Why?

❋ Can you say more about that?

❋ Wow, I never thought about it like that before!

❋ How did you know that?

❋ How could we check that thinking?

❋ Are there any other ways to think about that? What a thoughtful thinker you are!

❋ How did you figure that out? Can you tell us more about it?

❋ What do you know? How do you know it?

(Johnston, 2004); (Walther & Phillips, 2012)

SETTING THE SCENE

To create a classroom environment where children are empowered to grow as self-directed, independent learners, we need to know our end goals and structure the room's layout accordingly. There needs to be spaces where learners can interact with the teacher, with one another, and with books—lots of books! As our students grow, space is at a premium, but we keep certain priorities in mind when setting up our learning environment.

- **Designate a place for the classroom library.** Provide spaces for lots of fiction, informational, and poetry books. The classroom library can be centrally located or can be in several locations throughout the room, maybe different spots for different genres. It might be easiest to have your classroom library mirror a real library, where books are organized alphabetically by author. Just decide what works best for your students, you, and your space!

- **Choose a meeting area or place where your students can meet for whole-group instruction.** At the beginning of the year this helps us build community, and it helps maintain that community throughout the year. If space is at a premium, students may even stay at their desks during this time.

- **Provide a table for small-group work.** If space allows, we like to have a table or two in our classroom for small groups of students to work together. This is an area where students can meet for peer conferences or group work in a content area. It helps to keep some supplies here, such as sticky notes, pencils, blank/lined paper, and so on.

- **Design an area for conferring with individual readers and writers.** We recommend having a separate place to meet with students, stocked with student materials and forms for reading/writing conferences. To minimize distractions, it should be a quiet place away from where groups of students are working.

Transforming Literacy Teaching in the Era of Higher Standards, Grades 3–5 © 2015 by Karen Biggs-Tucker and Brian Tucker, Scholastic Teaching Resources

- **Organize an area or place where students can work with computers or other technology.** Whether it's desktops, laptops, or tablets, students can work together on projects in the same place, at the same time. You can also teach mini-lessons related to technology with small groups of students.

These are just some of the ideas to get you started setting up your learning environment. Remember that, given some of the instructional shifts in the new standards, having students talk with one another is essential. Make sure you have a space in your classroom that will encourage conversation among students, even if it is just a matter of grouping desks so that students have partners to talk to during a lesson. Our environment communicates to our students what is important to us.

Weave Content-Area Learning Experiences Throughout the Day

Our goal as intermediate teachers is to help our students build strong content knowledge. To do this, we need to continually integrate content-area knowledge into the school day. This helps students build connections in their learning while also providing a great time-management tool for teachers! The following are some ideas to consider as you begin planning your instruction for the year:

- **Plan thematic units centered on big ideas.** As you plan your science and social studies units, look for ways to integrate reading and writing into your instruction. For example, when looking for informational texts for teaching comprehension strategies or annotating during a close-reading lesson, use texts related to the topics that you are studying in social studies or science, if applicable. Or, for expository writing, think about having students research and write about topics they are studying in the content areas.

- **Integrate writing into math.** During your daily math instruction, look for ways for students to respond to math problems and demonstrate their thinking by writing responses. The new math standards offer many ways for students to demonstrate higher levels of critical thinking and problem solving. After fostering collaborative conversations between students in math workshop, especially during problem-solving experiences, we have them write about their thinking and reflect on how they have persevered or discovered a novel way of thinking about a math-problem solution.

- **Weave informational text and digital media resources into your reading and writing workshop.** We need to expose our students to a variety of informational texts during reading workshop. Students also need exposure to mentor texts to encourage them to write expository texts that include

Design a classroom library with many genres to meet the needs of student interests.

Establish locations where students can work together in partners or small groups.

Consider using tables instead of all desks.

Use technology to extend student learning.

Incorporate opportunities in math to allow students to show their problem-solving thinking through written responses.

information about school topics as well as topics that pertain to their daily lives.

Along with the standards for English language arts explored in this book, the Common Core Math Standards and Next Generation Science Standards provide clear content expectations. Although we will not be delving into the specifics of the standards for math and science, wise teachers know that it is essential to help learners see the connectedness of all of their learning. In Chapter 2, we will fully explore the similarities among the English language arts, math, and science practices to help you make these shared habits of mind a part of your classroom instruction every day.

Encourage Communication About a Variety of Topics for Various Audiences, Tasks, and Purposes

This book features a collection of teaching routines and experiences designed to foster your students' communication skills. To enhance this learning, call your students' attention to some of the routines you already have in place. Discuss and record the audience, task, and purpose for these routines, so that your students begin to understand how and why communication differs according the nature of these factors.

We find it helpful to create an anchor chart like the one on page 13 together and then refer back to it frequently throughout our learning day. It helps us in our conversations (both oral and written) as we communicate about our learning. Students can add other audiences, tasks, and purposes that they discover during their daily learning experiences.

We often assume that students understand the who, what, and why of communication in our everyday practice. But as we work with students daily, we realize that this is not always true. Referring to this chart is a practical, time-efficient way to remind them of what effective communication looks like.

Help Learners Understand, Accept, and Celebrate the Perspectives and Cultures of Others

As we walk into our classrooms each day, we see faces awaiting us, faces that represent a wide range of students with a wide range of learning styles and learning differences. As we transition to the new standards, how can we ensure the success of all of these students with their unique needs? They may be English language learners or students with cultural differences or special needs, but we know that it is their differences (and ultimately ours) that make us who we are, and we need to help our students learn to celebrate diversity.

Children's literature is a key resource for beginning the conversation about having empathy. Through their characters, books provide readers with both windows and mirrors. Many readers will recognize themselves when they see characters who look, feel, and have similar experiences as they do. More important, books provide readers with a window into the lives of others whose appearances and experiences are vastly different from their own. A few questions to ask readers in order to develop or assess empathy include the following:

- How would you feel if you experienced [the character's] life experiences? Why?

Facilitate opportunities for students to understand the cultures of others.

- How might you react if you experienced [an event/experience/adventure] that [the character] experienced? Why?
- What did the author want you to think/ feel/do after reading this book?

In *Opening Minds* (2012), Peter Johnston discusses the notion of social imagination by taking the concept of empathy to the next level and helping learners think about the "social-emotional logic that lies behind behavior" (p. 69). As we develop this capacity in our students, we have them participate in conversations about books that they have shared together so they can begin to think about not only how the character feels and acts, but also why the character feels and acts that way. We've included a few of our favorite books in the chart on page 14. As you read these books (or converse with readers about books they are independently reading), start conversations with students using the questions that follow:

We Communicate for Different Reasons

AUDIENCE (WHO?)	TASK (WHAT?)	PURPOSE (WHY?)
Me	Reading, writing, or researching independently	To develop my skills and become a better learner
My Teacher	Conferring with my teachers about my learning	To think and talk about my learning; to become a better learner
Peers	Conversing with other learners	To understand the thinking of others and how it relates to my own
The School Community	Participating in cross-grade-level learning experiences	To share my learning with others beyond our classroom
The Local Community	Inviting family, friends, and other community members to open houses where we share curricular presentations	To share our learning with others beyond our school

- How do you feel about what just happened in the book? Why?
- How do you think [the character] is feeling right now? What evidence from the text supports your thinking?
- How do you think the other characters in the book feel about [the character]? How would you feel about [the character]?
- Imagine what it might feel like to be [the character]. How are you feeling?
- Why do you think [the author] made [the character] say that?
- Why do you think [the author] made the other characters say that about [the character]?

HELP LEARNERS UNDERSTAND POINT OF VIEW

In order to help our soon-to-be-adolescent learners prepare for middle school and beyond, we need to help them see others' perspectives. This can be a challenge for our middle-grade learners, who are

A Few of Our Favorite Books About Developing Empathy and Social Awareness

Title, Author	Brief Summary
The Mitten Tree (Christiansen, 1997)	Sarah, an elderly woman, notices a young boy waiting for the bus without any mittens. She knits him a pair and hangs them on a spruce tree. It then becomes a tree that "gives" mittens to the needy children in the community.
Same, Same But Different (Kostecki-Shaw, 2011)	Elliot lives in America and Kailash lives in India. Through letters, they learn that their worlds are far more similar than they imagined.
Wonder (Palacio, 2012)	Auggie Pullman, who has been homeschooled his entire life because of a severe facial deformity, enters public school for the first time. He is met with both compassion and bullying, but he confronts it with courage that inspires others.
Under the Same Sun (Robinson, 2013)	Two families come together in Tanzania to celebrate Bibi's 85th birthday. When it is time to return to America, Bibi reminds them that no matter where they are, they are always "under the same sun."
Each Kindness (Woodson, 2012)	When Maya moves to town and arrives at school, Chloe chooses not to be her friend because she doesn't look like the other girls. One day Chloe decides to take a chance and be Maya's friend. Is she too late?

Johnston (2012) reminds us that there are several markers that should be in place in classrooms to help students critique others and be critiqued in thoughtful literacy conversations. Students should be:

❋ ready to appreciate the differences that appear in the classroom every day, among their peers and in activities and thinking perspectives.

❋ ready to understand one another's varying perspectives.

❋ able to question the assumptions of others on a particular issue.

❋ ready to listen to others' points of view on a topic.

often focused on themselves and their own lives. Now that we have laid the foundation for creating an environment of empathy and open-mindedness for our students, we are ready to help them recognize and appreciate that different people see the world in different ways. This can be a challenging, but ultimately powerful, concept as learners begin to look beyond their own experiences and think about those of others.

When discussing texts or topics with varying or multiple viewpoints, you can ask students questions that help them recognize points of view that differ from their own.

- What are the different points of view or perspectives in this text?

- How might this text (or topic) look from a different perspective or point of view?

- How is my perspective or point of view similar to or different from those of the characters in the text?

Develop Open-Mindedness to Help Students Critique as Well as Comprehend

The new standards ask students to critique text in addition to understanding it. As students develop these skills, they must begin to open up their minds to the thinking of others. This is an important ability as students begin to move from the isolated process of internal comprehension to the more public process of interactive comprehension, in which readers share their thinking with others to develop and refine ideas. As they ask questions, share multiple perspectives, and search for text evidence to support their ideas, students have the opportunity to articulate their thinking before writing a reading response.

Part of this process is asking and answering critical questions. We must teach students to interact in a thoughtful and respectful manner so their discussions are productive. For ideas on how to help students with this task, we again turn to the work of Peter Johnston (2012), which we have summarized in the box at right.

One way to develop students' ability to be open-minded about their reading, writing, and thinking is to always ask, "What do you think?" and "Why do you think that?" Taking time in our classroom conversations to model valuing the thought process, not only the answers, encourages students to share their thinking and not be afraid of giving a wrong answer. This takes time for both teachers and students to get used to. Learning to ask open-ended questions helps students learn to be open-minded.

Remember that developing open-mindedness doesn't happen overnight for our students. Be patient with your learners as well as with yourself as you practice these skills in daily conversations.

Value Evidence

The higher standards ask students to critique the information that they come in contact with in school. When they are presented with a claim that someone has made, either through writing or speaking, students need to consider the following questions:

- Who is making this claim? What makes this person credible?
- What is the evidence to support this person's claim?
- What other positions or perspectives are there that relate to the claim?
- How can I compare and contrast these different views, think about the biases and assumptions behind them, weigh their warrants, and come to an evidence-based, well-reasoned stance?

(Calkins, Ehrenworth, and Lehman, 2012, p. 10).

Create a classroom environment where students value the thinking of others.

Some ideas to get students thinking and ready to listen to one another's perspectives:

❋ Ask open-ended questions—questions that have multiple answers (no one "right" answer).

❋ Use words like *maybe, perhaps,* and *I wonder* in conversations to get students thinking.

❋ Use wait time to get students thinking.

❋ Do not judge ideas. Let students critiques themselves and their peers.

❋ Always have students sit so that they can make eye contact when having "critiquing conversations." Have a small group of students sit in a circle so they can make eye contact as they talk to one another.

(Johnston, 2012)

The classroom strategies in this chapter will help our students become critical thinkers. We also need to reinforce the habit of supporting thinking with evidence, whether it is evidence that readers have found in text or through personal experience, rather than just thinking supported by feelings or emotions.

In addition, we need to model the important habit of evidence-based thinking in our professional lives. By providing research-based rationale for our practice to administrators, parents, and other stakeholders, we demonstrate that we value evidence-based thinking. Our actions, whether we realize it or not, are being viewed by our learners and ultimately impact their learning behaviors. On the next page, you will find "A Portrait of an Accomplished Teacher." Notice how it mirrors "A Portrait of a

A Portrait of an Accomplished Teacher

✷ Independently seeks out self-directed professional learning experiences.

✷ Actively participates in professional learning communities.

✷ Builds strong content-area knowledge.

✷ Adjusts instruction based on students' interests and learning needs.

✷ Analyzes as well as critiques his or her own teaching practices.

✷ Values evidence and uses data to make instructional decisions.

✷ Seeks to understand the perspectives and cultures of students, students' families, and colleagues.

✷ Evaluates other points of view critically and constructively.

✷ Uses technology and digital media strategically and capably.

Adapted from Common Core State Standards (CCSS) for English Language Arts (NGA Center and CCSSO, 2010, p.7)

Ways to Integrate Technology Into Learning Experiences

Students can:

✷ write a blog post about books they are reading or a topic they are learning about

✷ create a wiki to record and share learning about a science or social studies topic

✷ make a podcast of a favorite poem or scene from a play

✷ develop an online poster using an app such as Glogster to show learning of a self-selected subject related to a favorite book or content-area topic

Learner Who Meets the Common Core Standards" on which this chapter was based. As we look to transform our own teaching practices, it makes sense that our own outcomes should reflect the outcomes that we desire for our students. To help reach these goals, we've provided a few helpful tips for staying current with the evidence-based practices in the box on page 17.

Creating a learning community that values empathy, social awareness, multiple points of view, and evidence-based thinking can feel daunting. However, it can be done successfully as you implement the foregoing ideas consistently over time.

Use Technology to Enhance Student Learning

Many classroom teachers have a love/hate relationship with the technology we work with on a daily basis. Depending on the available technology and our level of knowledge about that technology, many teachers feel challenged by how to effectively integrate it into the curriculum. We, too, have struggled to find meaningful ways for students to use technology to extend their learning in reading, writing, math, science, and social studies.

The standards recognize the importance of technology as our students move into a society saturated with digital media. Our students often know as much (or more) about the technology in our classrooms as we do. We no longer need to use technology as a tool to engage them (although for some students it can be a great motivator), but it is an important means of extending and enhancing literacy learning and should be integrated into learning experiences throughout the day.

Keeping Current With Evidence-Based Practices

❋ Be an active reader, writer, and thinker. Always be reading a book and talking to your students about what you are reading; keep a "Books I've Read" list and a "Someday" list. Keep a reader's and a writer's notebook. Share with students what you are reading, writing, and thinking about. It is important for them to see you living a reader's and a writer's life, too!

❋ Start a teacher's notebook. Purchase a small notebook to record your thinking and reflections. You can organize it by adding sticky tabs labeled with the following categories:

- Observations
- Discussions/Charts
- Books
- Things to Do
- Notes from professional development sessions

(This is also a great way to grow professionally and share your thinking with colleagues in your learning community.)

❋ Engage in discussions of professional books as well as other texts. Find colleagues with similar philosophies. Meet, talk, share, reflect, argue, debate, and learn together. Join Twitter, Facebook, Pinterest, or other social media platforms where you can network with other teachers who share your passion for teaching.

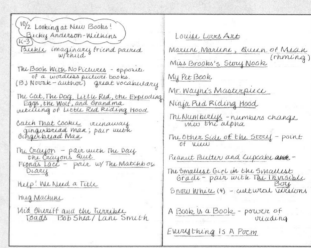

Start a teacher's notebook to record thinking and reflections.

As you look at your own practice, think about how you are already using technology and ask yourself if students are using it for more than just playing games. The standards ask students to use digital resources to gather information and then communicate that information to others.

Moving On

Regardless of the current season, you're probably already thinking about something that you'd like to improve in your classroom practice. It's probably related to the implementation of the new standards, but it may pertain to reading or writing workshop, or just improving your literacy instruction. We have found that the best way to do this is to just move. You know: make a change, even a small change. The small changes can make a big difference for our learners over time, and they are easy to implement. So look for the small changes you can make. Whether it means changing the way you communicate with your students, moving a bookshelf, reorganizing your classroom library, or implementing a content-area teaching strategy, it is never too late to start moving! What will you do tomorrow to nudge learning forward in your classroom?

Chapter 2

Discovering Connections

Streamlining Our Instruction

If you've been teaching for a few years, you've experienced the frustration of trying to pack all your reading and writing instruction into one school year. We've found ourselves getting to the end of the school year and looking at the laundry list of standards that we were expected to cover with our students and feeling inadequate because we were not able to get it all done. For example, our previous state standards in Illinois for English language arts had more than 100 performance descriptors for each grade level. These included the skills that each grade-level teacher was to teach, not to mention the skills or strategies students needed to be retaught to fill in gaps in their learning. When we were feeling overwhelmed and frustrated, we often wondered how our students must be feeling as we pushed and pulled them through the year's curriculum,

We breathed a sigh of relief when the new standards came on the scene. This document essentially presented ten standards for reading, ten for writing, and six for speaking and listening. (Yes, there are additional foundational standards and language standards, but those were relatively easy to integrate with the reading and writing standards.) The standards looked like an opportunity to streamline our instruction and a chance to teach, and ultimately reteach, the standards multiple times throughout the

> Go online to view a video on Standards Integration in Action. See page 160 for details.

year. The integrated nature of these standards helps teachers with our planning and with communicating the purpose of those standards to students. Because they include reading, writing, speaking, and listening, the standards remind teachers to include all the important components in our lessons. Also, the structure and design of the standards help us to focus our thinking (and planning) on the big ideas that the standards contain.

Focus on Key Concepts

The interrelated nature of the standards helps streamline instruction, allowing us to focus on one key concept and apply it to different learning contexts. This helps us in our daily planning of both reading and writing instruction. For example, when planning experiences where students are comparing and contrasting texts (either fiction or informational), you might model the thinking process in a shared read-aloud. Then, during writing workshop, students can compare and contrast pieces written by themselves or their classmates. Finally, in social studies and science, students can compare textbook selections and the information presented on topics of study. Focusing on these key concepts and building connections between them helps strengthen learning for our students. Our first step is to look at the connections among the standards for reading, writing, speaking, and listening.

We would encourage you to consider posting the key concepts at right somewhere in your classroom where both you and your students can easily refer to them and keeping them in your lesson plan book. This helps remind us of what is most important as we plan our reading and writing workshops. Our lesson planning often begins and ends with one question: "Does this literacy lesson, routine, or habit lead students to independently apply these key concepts?" If it does, then we forge ahead; if not, we reevaluate the activity or (Dare we say it?) transform it to meet the needs of our 21st-century learners.

We also integrate this language into our workshop as we set the purposes for our lessons. This is a good way for our students to understand what the key concepts are and what they mean to their individual learning. It is also helpful to consider the connections between the hallmarks of proficient readers and listeners with those of proficient writers and speakers. Carol Fuhler and Maria Walther (2007) share these descriptors, which align neatly with the key ideas contained in the standards. Examining these connections and how they connect with our daily teaching has proven helpful to us as we design our literacy lessons.

Key Concepts for Learners in Grades 3–5

* Read closely to understand
* Write to communicate to different audiences and for a variety of purposes
* Use textual evidence to support thinking
* Converse with others, enriching one another's thinking
* Make logical inferences to support understanding of text
* Refer to details and examples while explaining thinking
* Consider themes, central messages, and morals
* Compare and contrast varying points of view
* Analyze the purpose of the writer or speaker
* Notice and use different approaches to crafting text
* Evaluate the writer's and/or speaker's message
* Apply new learning to a variety of contexts

How the Standards Help Streamline Your Instruction

They:

* contain fewer standards than traditional state standards.
* allow more time to revisit standards throughout the year.
* focus on essential understandings.
* promote integration of language arts in content areas throughout the day.
* create opportunities for student-driven learning through research and use of technology.

Take into account the hallmarks of proficient literacy learners.

Cultivate Habits of Mind

If you are like us, you know and believe in the adage that the more you integrate throughout your day, the better. But we also know that this is often easier said than done. In the next section, we've synthesized and aligned practices from math and science, then matched them to our own ELA practices to show how they are focused on the same key concepts. We hope you will see the common thought processes embedded in all the standards that we can model, demonstrate, and foster in our learners throughout.the learning day.

We started by unpacking the Standards for Mathematical Practices (NGA Center and CCSSO, 2010, pp. 6–7). As we looked at these practices carefully, we noticed certain practices that we wanted to cultivate in our students, not only during math time but throughout

Hallmarks of Proficient Literacy Learners

Proficient Readers/Listeners	Proficient Writers/Speakers
Construct meaning while actively reading or listening by integrating and applying comprehension strategies and asking clarifying questions.	Convey meaning through writing or speaking by integrating and applying writing strategies and asking questions to ensure the clarity of the message.
Search for text-based evidence to support their understanding of the message.	Provide text-based evidence to support their communication of the message.
Adjust their reading based on the purpose, type of text, and, ultimately, the audience for the text.	Design their written work to match their purpose, audience, task, and content.
Activate their schema and build background knowledge for a wide variety of texts and utilize that schema to help them better understand their reading.	Collaborate with real authors through authentic reading of mentor texts— learning about written and oral texts that can extend their own thinking as aspiring authors.
Develop an understanding of how words work and how authors use them to enhance text. (foundational skills)	Expand their vocabulary through words learned through reading and listening to books.
Use decoding or fix-up strategies flexibly to make meaning from unfamiliar words.	Apply strategies and utilize resources to figure out how to spell unknown words while writing.
Clarify the meaning of the vocabulary in the books they read or hear.	Choose precise, engaging words for the reader/listener when they write/speak.
Use emerging knowledge of the conventions of standard English and grammar to better understand the ideas of others.	Use knowledge of the conventions and rules of standard English and grammar when writing/speaking.
Read with fluency and expression.	Write and speak with fluency and expression.

Adapted from Literature Is Back! *(Fuhler & Walther, 2007)*

the day. These were enduring habits of mind that would lead our students to be successful learners. For example, when students show perseverance in math, we know that this habit of mind will aid them in scientific inquiry and foster lifelong literacy. As we make those connections as teachers, we help our learners make those same important connections. We then noticed that these same habits of mind were mirrored in the Next Generation Science Standards for Science and Engineering Practices (NGSS Lead States, 2013). We simplified things by creating parallel literacy practices. This way, instead of looking at three sets of separate practices, you have one set for easy reference. Our hope is that these will come to color the ways in which your students think, act, and

Build in literacy opportunities throughout the day.

converse throughout the day. In math, science, and engineering, we have moved the emphasis away from just getting a right answer and the rote memorization of facts to thinking about the *practices* students can learn from solving a mathematical problem, posing a scientific inquiry, or defining an engineering problem. Similarly, in literacy we help learners discover what enduring understanding they can develop by comprehending a text or communicating with others. See the chart on pages 22–24 for further explanation. To assist you as you make your own connections among these standards, you will find multi-genre text sets related to grades 3–5 science topics on page 41. Here are some of our favorite picture books to enhance your math experiences.

Recommended Read-Alouds for Enhancing Math Understanding

Title, Author	Brief Summary
The Boy Who Loved Math: The Improbable Life of Paul Erdös (Heiligman, 2013)	Hungarian mathematician Paul Erdos loved math as a child. Although he struggled to do simple household chores, he traveled around the world collaborating with other mathematicians.
Edgar Allan Poe's Pie: Math Puzzlers in Classic Poems (Lewis, 2012)	This collection of classic poems has a little math woven in to hook readers.
Lifetime: The Amazing Numbers in Animal Lives (Schaefer, 2013)	In this interesting twist on the traditional counting book, readers learn how many antlers a caribou grows and the number of babies a male seahorse has in its lifetime.
Swirl by Swirl: Spirals in Nature (Sidman, 2011)	This study of the repetition of swirls in nature shows when and where they appear, as well as their beauty.
Ten Birds (Young, 2011)	A combination counting book and fable about problem solving. Does the "brilliant" bird have the best solution for getting across a river? Maybe not.

Our Questions About Animals

- What do they look like? (physical features)
- How big are they? (physical features)
- What do they eat and what eats them? (food chain)
- What color are they? (physical features)
- Where do they live? (habitat)
- How do they have babies? (life cycle)
- What types or species are there? (classification)
- How long do they live? (life cycle)
- How do they communicate with each other? (communication)
- What behaviors do they have within their communities? (behaviors)

Guide learners as they generate questions about a topic.

Common Core Standards for Mathematical Practice	The Next Generation Science Standards: Standards for Science and Engineering Practices (3–5)	Karen and Brian's Standards for Literacy Practices (adapted from Walther, 2015)
Make sense of problems and persevere in solving them (MP.1) Students who are proficient mathematicians know that they must first make sense of a problem before they can solve it. One way that they make sense of it is to think of other problems that may be similar to it. These students often solve problems creatively. When presented with a challenging problem, expert problem solvers do not give up. Instead, they ask themselves, "How can I make sense of this problem?" "What strategies can I use to help me keep going and ultimately solve it?"	**Make sense of the scientific problems in the world and persevere in solving them** Science students at the intermediate level ask questions and define problems about the world around them. Based on their questions, they create investigations that they use to solve those problems or answer their questions. These investigations demand that they persevere. They ask themselves, "What can I learn about the world around me?" "What can I do to figure that out?" *(Adapted from Practice #1 Asking Questions and Defining Problems)*	**Make sense of complex text and persevere in figuring it out** Proficient readers make sense of increasingly complex text by using a variety of strategies. They confirm their understanding of text by self-monitoring their comprehension. They ask questions such as, "Does this make sense to me?" "If it does not, what can I do to help me understand it?" They also recognize that as text becomes more complex, they must display perseverance in making sense of it.
Reason abstractly and quantitatively (MP.2) Students who are proficient problem solvers have a variety of strategies that they use to solve problems. They understand the relationships between abstract data and quantitative data. They understand not only how quantitative data relates to computation, but also to the meaning of a unit within the problem and in the answer.	**Reason analytically and interpret patterns and relationships** Students collect data through observation and measurement, and share their findings with their peers. When they are able to use their observations and other data to support their investigation, they demonstrate analytical thinking. *(Adapted from Practice #4 Analyzing and Interpreting Data)*	**Reason abstractly and qualitatively** Learners can understand, problem solve, and plan based on information gained from texts and/or images. Using qualitative reasoning means students can attend to the meaning of the words, not just how to decode the words.

Common Core Standards for Mathematical Practice	The Next Generation Science Standards: Standards for Science and Engineering Practices (3–5)	Karen and Brian's Standards for Literacy Practices (adapted from Walther, 2015)
Construct viable arguments and critique the reasoning of others (MP.3) Learners in the intermediate grades can demonstrate how they solve problems. They can explain their thinking to their peers and "defend" their thinking to others. Doing so allows students to confirm or revise their thinking.	**Construct and recognize evidence-based arguments and critique the reasoning of others** Learners in a scientific community need to understand the difference between evidence-based arguments and opinions. Science students are able to recognize and ultimately construct their own evidence-based arguments. They also must be able to recognize evidence-based arguments and opinions in others' reasoning. *(Adapted from Practice #7 Engaging in Argument from Evidence)*	**Construct logical, evidence-based arguments and critique the reasoning of others** Skilled readers and writers use information from a variety of sources to create evidence-based arguments. In collaborative conversations with their peers, they are able to not only share their own arguments but to critique the arguments of their peers. Based on mutual feedback, learners develop the ability to confirm or revise their original thinking, often returning to the text for more information or support for their thinking.
Model with mathematics (MP.4) Skilled mathematicians use a variety of models to share their thinking with others, such as tables, graphs, and diagrams. The ability to create and use them to explain their thinking is an important skill for learners to have as part of the problem-solving process.	**Develop and use models** During scientific investigation, students create and use models appropriate for the purpose. They ask themselves, "How will this model help me better understand or help me gather information about my investigation?" *(Adapted from Practice #2 Developing and Using Models)*	**Think by writing** Readers extend their understanding of what they read by writing. Writing about fiction and informational text helps deepen comprehension while connecting to other learning derived from previously read texts. Learners ask themselves, "How can I communicate my understanding of my reading to help myself as a reader?" and "How can I communicate what I have read with others?"
Use appropriate tools strategically (MP.5) A proficient mathematician needs to think strategically as to the best tool to use in a given problem-solving situation, whether it is a pencil and paper, ruler, compass, calculator, or computer. Knowing each tool's advantages and disadvantages helps the student know which one suits the job . . . or if one is needed at all!	**Use mathematical and computational thinking strategically** Learners strategically use mathematical and computational data for their scientific investigation. They select the data to be used based on what is best for the scientific problem. *(Adapted from Practice #5 Using Mathematical and Computational Thinking)*	**Use structures of text, text features, and digital resources strategically** To better understand complex texts, students examine how the text is structured. They use their understanding of text structure to better comprehend what they read. They ask themselves, "How does text structure help me predict what the text will be about?" and "How can I use what I know about text structures to help me better understand what I'm reading?"

Common Core Standards for Mathematical Practice	The Next Generation Science Standards: Standards for Science and Engineering Practices (3–5)	Karen and Brian's Standards for Literacy Practices (adapted from Walther, 2015)
Attend to precision (MP.6) Mathematicians make sure that their answers are both accurate and precise. Skilled students can explain their mathematical thinking clearly and concisely to their classmates. To do this, they must understand their own internal processes and give carefully worded explanations to others about their thinking.	**Construct explanations and design solutions** Scientists create a variety of design solutions based on the investigations that they are completing. They choose the best method for the purpose of the investigation that they are conducting, and they present and explain their designs to one another. They also explain how the design would help lead to solution to the investigation for which it would be implemented. *(Adapted from Practice #6 Constructing Explanations and Designing Solutions)*	**Comprehend and communicate with precision** As proficient readers comprehend increasingly complex texts, they must monitor their comprehension with precision. Whether they are confirming or revising a prediction or making an inference based on information found in the text, readers must attend to the meanings (both literal and implied) within the text they are reading. In addition, as they are communicating with others (both orally and in writing) they must share their thoughts precisely so that others can understand their thinking about what they have read.
Look for and make use of structure (MP.7) *and* **Look for and express regularity in repeated reasoning (MP.8)** Expert mathematicians use the structure of the problems themselves to make sense of and solve the problems successfully. They also use the patterns and relationships depicted in the problems to help solve them. Both the structure and the patterns become an important part of the problem-solving process, and also an important part of checking their work and final answer for reasonableness.	**Look for and make use of structure** Scientists use observation, formulas, and other processes to help them create patterns in the queries that they are solving. Finding these patterns helps them develop the models needed during experiments or the design process.	**Look for and make use of structure and express regularity in repeated reasoning** Literacy learners use the structures in a variety of texts that they read to help them make sense of their reading; this ultimately helps them understand those texts. They also look for meanings within the texts to help them comprehend what they have read, especially as the texts become more complex. Experienced readers use reasoning as a form of self-monitoring to help them know when they are comprehending text and when their comprehension breaks down. When this happens, they know they need to create a plan to help them get back on track to understanding their reading.

Build in self-reflection time for students to help make connections between learning experiences.

Again, the goal here is to gain an understanding of the similarities between these standards and the practices embedded within them. Remember when we said that it was important to integrate the standards throughout the day? This allows you to think about how to do so effectively and efficiently for your students. Building those connections for students in one content area helps strengthen their learning in all content areas. For example, consider how many times you have students ask questions for a purpose in a variety of content areas. In reading workshop, readers ask questions to give them a purpose for their independent reading; in math, you ask questions about problems to find an accurate solution. Later, scientists ask questions for research purposes. As teachers, it takes only a brief moment to help students make connections between those learning experiences by saying, "We asked a variety of questions today! Can someone share a time when you asked a question and how it helped you as a learner?" Building in this self-reflection allows students to begin to make connections for themselves between the learning they are doing throughout their day. We were amazed at the difference this made in our students' learning. The best part for us was that it only took a few minutes of reflection time at the end of the day to do this. This is ultimately what we are trying to do as we integrate our instruction!

SYNTHESIZING LEARNING TARGETS

As we take a moment to reflect on all the practices and think about the students to whom we will deliver those practices tomorrow, we have a bit of an anxiety attack. We assume that you feel the same way too. When we feel this way, we first find a paper bag to take a few deep breaths into. Then we take a step back, and when we are feeling a bit more rational, we think about ways to simplify things.

After reading these pages, we hope that you have a better understanding of each of the individual practices. You can communicate these to your learners by using the learning targets in the box at right.

These targets have been invaluable to us in our classroom as we focus students on the behaviors found within the practices themselves. We like to begin with perseverance. It is a foundational target for our students, and it helps them prepare for the challenges that await them—not only when they are with us, but for the future

> ❋ I can PAUSE.
>
> ❋ I can PONDER.
>
> ❋ I can look for PATTERNS.
>
> ❋ I can look to PROBLEM SOLVE.
>
> ❋ I can look to be PRECISE.
>
> ❋ I can communicate my PROCESS.
>
> ❋ I can PERSEVERE.
>
> *(Walther, 2015)*

as well. It also helps those students who need to be done first and those who have to get it done perfectly. To model perseverance, we begin by discussing characters in books and other media who have demonstrated this characteristic. Then we look for opportunities to connect these situations to times during the learning day where perseverance occurs. Whether it means sticking with a complex text, solving a challenging math problem, or researching a science topic, perseverance is the key to success!

Text Set of Picture Books With Characters Who Persevere

Title, Author	Brief Summary
Rosie Revere, Engineer (Beaty, 2013) *Iggy Peck, Architect* (Beaty, 2007)	A pair of texts that celebrate the creativity and ingenuity of young inventors everywhere. These characters were encouraged and inspired by loved ones to follow their dreams.
Bridget's Beret (Lichtenheld, 2010)	Bridget's beret provides her with inspiration when she does her artwork. But then her beret goes missing. Will she be able to continue her art or will she be done with it forever?
The Girl Who Made Mistakes (Pett, 2011)	Beatrice does everything perfectly, and she always wins the talent show. Then, one day, the unthinkable happens. What will happen to Beatrice and her record of perfection?

Title, Author	Brief Summary
Clara and Davie (Polacco, 2014)	Clara loves animals and cares for them in a special way. With the encouragement of her brother, Davie, Clara begins caring for other people. This is the story of Clara Barton, who grew up to start the American Red Cross.
Going Places (Reynolds & Reynolds, 2014)	In the Going Places go-cart race, every kid gets the same kit. Maya decides to do something a little bit different with the help of a friend. Will teamwork pay off?
The Most Magnificent Thing (Spires, 2014)	A young girl and her best friend, who happens to be a dog, decide to make something magnificent. But she soon discovers that it isn't as easy as she thought.

We've discovered the connections among the English language arts standards for reading, writing, listening, and speaking. We've synthesized the practices that learners use in math and science and as and citizens of a literate society. Next, we'll consider how science and engineering practices align with writing standards and how you can integrate the writing standards into your science instruction or visa versa.

INTEGRATE INVESTIGATING, RESEARCHING, AND WRITING

One of the most effective ways we have found to integrate our reading/writing instruction with content-area practices is through student inquiry. In *Comprehension and Collaboration: Inquiry Circles in Action* (2009), Stephanie Harvey and Harvey Daniels define the inquiry approach to teaching by identifying the following three key strands:

- Framing school study around questions developed and shaped by students

- Handing the brainwork of learning back to the students

- Focusing on the development of students' thinking, first, foremost, and always (pp. 56–57)

Encourage and support students as they investigate, research, and write.

Inquiry-based student research is one of the most effective instructional practices that we have found. A combination of reading workshop, writing workshop, and content-area workshop, this method allows students to immerse themselves in units that encourage them to investigate, research, and write. It also enables teachers to promote a wide range of skills that support students as readers, writers, and critical thinkers within the structure of workshop and content-area instructional time.

With the need to familiarize students with the content that they will be researching during the inquiry-based experiences in limited instructional time, it makes sense to incorporate reading and writing into science/social studies workshop as they investigate their inquiry research topics.

If you take a moment to read through the Next Generation Science Practices 3 and 8 and compare them with the ELA Writing Standards 7 and 8, you will discover that they share the following expectations for students' learning:

- Participate in shared or collaborative investigations or research to answer questions or support their thinking

- Gather information from multiple sources, such as texts, images, investigations, or experiences, to answer a question or solve a problem

- Synthesize information from multiple sources, such as texts, images, investigations, or experiences, to answer a question or solve a problem

- Evaluate different ways to observe and measure, or different sources, to determine the best way or resource to help answer the question

- Communicate new information or ideas orally or in writing using details, such as models, drawings, and/or text features, to support thinking

If we want our students to be self-directed and independent learners, we have to create learning opportunities where they can investigate their own questions or test out their own theories and ideas. As difficult as it may sound and as challenging as it may be to manage, we must step outside of our comfort zones and let our students take these steps to understanding. Our ultimate goal is for our students to leave our classrooms ready to be the problem solvers that the real world will require them to be. We need to give them the skills, strategies, and confidence to solve those problems through the inquiry process. How, then, do we set up those learning experiences? We believe the solution lies in refocusing some of our current teaching practices to transform them into inquiry experiences.

Create opportunities where students can investigate their own questions, theories, and ideas.

Transform Teaching Routines and Create Inquiry Experiences

Along with reading, writing, listening, and speaking skills, literacy instruction must also foster the skills of fluency, word recognition, grammar, and mechanics. For this reason, our current instructional repertoire includes several research-based routines like the ones that follow on page 28.

In the next three chapters, we will examine each of these routines and suggest ways of transforming them. By changing the focus along with the language, questions, and conversations that surround the routine, we can nudge students toward independence. In this day of high-stakes

The Four Stages of Small-Group Inquiry

IMMERSE	INVESTIGATE
• Invite curiosity	• Develop questions
• Build background	• Search for information
• Find topics	• Discover answers
• Wonder	

COALESCE	GO PUBLIC
• Intensify research	• Share learning
• Synthesize information	• Demonstrate understanding
• Build knowledge	• Take action

(Harvey & Daniels, 2009, pp. 61–62)

Reading Workshop Routines	Writing Workshop Routines
• Read-Aloud	• Reading Like a Writer
• Think-Aloud (reading demonstrations)	• Think-Aloud (writing demonstrations)
• Mini-Lessons	• Mini-Lessons
• Shared Reading	• Shared Writing
• Reader's Notebook	• Writer's Notebook
• Independent Reading	• Independent Writing

Recognize the importance of talk in the social nature of learning in the workshop setting.

Provide ways students can investigate questions or test hypotheses throughout the learning day.

testing, many districts have put aside the knowledge and expertise of teachers. Instead, out of desperation, they hand teachers packaged programs designed to prepare students for "the test." The test preparation students receive denies them the opportunity to think independently, creatively, or critically. In our opinion, it is counterproductive. If we were in charge of the education world (and someday we hope to be!), we'd reallocate all of the funds spent on those programs for quality professional development for teachers and lots of good books for students. Luckily, you've already decided to engage in your own personal professional development by reading this book, and you'll soon learn how to transform the above teaching routines and add another layer on top: inquiry experiences.

Planning an inquiry experience begins with a question: "What do I want my students to know and be able to do after the experience?" Each learning experience can, and should, be repeated over the course of the year with increasingly more complex texts or ideas. These inquiry experiences are not one-and-done lessons to check off a list. Rather they comprise a way of teaching the standards that is authentic and integrated into your daily instruction. In addition to the inquiry experiences, your teaching routines will be strengthening literacy learning in your classroom by providing the practice that readers and writers need to experience throughout the year. Next, you'll see where the Transforming Teaching charts will come in handy. In Part 2, we'll show you how you can refine your teaching routines and create inquiry experiences to better align with the standards, thinking practices, and community-building ideas we've already discussed.

Utilize Formative Assessment

As you transform your teaching practices, you can further strengthen them and help students master the more rigorous standards by incorporating formative assessment. Formative assessment is a powerful partner in this process because it helps you gain a better understanding of the students' understandings and/or misconceptions. It lets you give the descriptive feedback students need to move forward, and it helps students begin to assess and reflect on their own learning.

In the many years that we've struggled with assessing learners, we've come to believe that we make it harder than it needs to be by forgetting what the ultimate purpose of assessment really is. The word *assess* derives from the Greek word meaning "to sit beside." This is a wonderful reminder to us that if we take the time to sit with our students and listen to them, they will tell us what we need to know about them as learners. So now we make a point of stopping to ask an important question whenever we face the task of assessing our students: "What is the purpose of the assessment?" In order to do this, we need to ask ourselves three important questions: Where do I want this learner to end up? Where is the student right now? And how can I close the learning gap? (Chappuis, 2009). To answer the first question, we look to the "Portrait of a Learner" in Chapter 1, along with the specific standards to support that learner for each grade level. The answer to the second question is found in the formative data that we collect on each student through anecdotal notes, observational notes, and anything that gives us insight into how the student is performing, focusing on specific strengths and weaknesses. The answer to the third question is the teacher's instructional response. We use information that we find in books and design best-practice instruction that moves students toward success in literacy.

In "Formative Assessment: Simply, No Additives" (Roskos & Neuman, 2012), the authors provide the following helpful tips for teachers who may be new to the process:

- Choose multi-level learning activities that involve multi-learner as well as teacher-student interactions.
- Embed key concepts (ideas or learning standards to master) and skills (procedures or strategies essential to performance) in the content of the activity.
- Determine success criteria for the activity using a rubric or checklist (whenever possible, create these collaboratively with students).

Integrate read-aloud experiences to scaffold learning in all subjects.

The Characteristics of Inquiry Experiences

❋ Deepen students' ability to integrate and apply reading, writing, thinking, listening, and speaking skills

❋ Expand learners' understanding of the world

❋ Encourage inquiry, uncertainty, risk-taking, and perseverance

❋ Develop agency, also known as an "I can do this myself" attitude

❋ Emphasize text-based evidence to support ideas, thinking, and writing

❋ Foster understanding of complex texts and ideas

❋ Integrate technology for authentic purposes

❋ Promote engaged learning

(Walther, 2015)

Standards for Literacy Practices

❋ Make sense of complex text and persevere in figuring it out

❋ Reason abstractly and *qualitatively*

❋ Construct logical, evidence-based arguments and critique the reasoning of others

❋ Think by writing

❋ Use structures of text, text features, and digital resources strategically

❋ Comprehend and communicate with precision

❋ Look for and make use of structure

(Walther, 2015)

Coach, guide, and give students descriptive feedback.

The Steps to Creating Inquiry Experiences

❈ Determine learning targets to lead students toward key standards-based learning

❈ Select the experience that best meets the target and matches your students' needs

❈ Demonstrate, coach, guide, observe, give descriptive feedback, take anecdotal notes, and collect formative data

❈ Reflect and repeat!

(Walther, 2015)

- Create a schedule or plan for completing assessments.
- Start slowly, adding activities as your confidence and expertise with formative assessment grows. (Our addition based on our own experiences over the years!)

IDENTIFY LEARNING TARGETS

In Part 2, we've identified some learning targets for each teaching routine and inquiry experience. We find it helpful to redefine each learning target in student-friendly language, especially when we are doing goal setting with students. Creating "I can" statements is one way to make the standards more "user-friendly" both for you and your students. These statements help clarify the purpose of the lesson and can aide you in creating checklists to assess student learning after the lesson. Once you have your goals and have identified how you are going to teach them to your students, you can begin to think about how you are going to check their understanding, both formally and informally, throughout your learning experiences.

CHECK FOR UNDERSTANDING

By the end of the first day of school, you probably know a lot about your students: who will be your hard workers, your pleasers, and yes, even your troublemakers! We glean this information through a variety of observational and formative assessment tools. Based on what you learn about your students, you then develop a plan to meet their needs. The good news is that you can use those same skills that you used on Day 1 to assess students throughout the year.

Big Ideas About Formative Assessment

❈ Formative assessment is an ongoing process

❈ Formative assessment will help you answer the following questions critical to effective literacy instruction:

- What are my students' strengths and weaknesses?
- What specific, descriptive feedback should I give each learner?
- What adjustments should I make to my instruction?

❈ Formative assessment meets your students' needs to maximize both motivation and achievement. Through your interactions with students, you are guiding them to ask these questions:

- Where am I now?
- Where am I going?
- How can I get there?

(Chappuis, 2009, p. 9)

A Few Ways to Check Student Understanding

* Take notes on sticky notes as students discuss their thinking aloud; place the notes in your teaching notebook.

* Record students' thinking and ideas on anchor charts or have them record their own thinking on sticky notes to create class anchor charts.

* Utilize written exit slips to assess student thinking.

* Analyze students' written responses in reader's notebooks or learning logs.

* Utilize technology tools, such as Evernote or Confer apps, as a note-taking tool during reading and writing conferences.

Looking Back, Moving Forward

In Chapter 1, you learned the conditions that work together to create a learning environment where agency and independence are cultivated and celebrated. Here, in Chapter 2, we added a layer to those conditions by examining the intertwining of content area standards, the definition of teaching routines and learning experiences, and the role formative assessment plays in the development of a learner. Let's move forward by revisiting two learning contexts, reading workshop (Chapter 3) and writing workshop (Chapter 4) to integrate what we've learned and elevate and enhance these research-based structures.

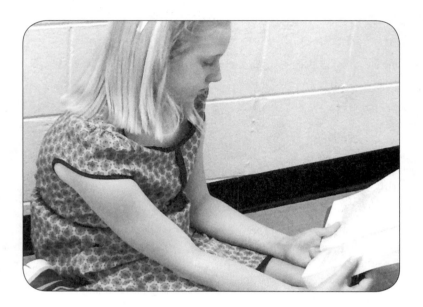

Elevating Reading Workshop

Creating a Lifelong Love of Books!

We celebrated our tenth wedding anniversary this summer, and it's hard to believe that we've been married that long. Many of our interests are separate and unique to each of us (Brian enjoys video games, and Karen is inclined to watch reality television), but there is one that we share: books! We love to go to bookstores (especially independent booksellers) and buy books. In fact, we have so many books at home and at school that we often lose track of them and buy duplicates. (That's OK. Our son is now a teacher, and he is always eager to take our extras and add them to his growing classroom library.)

It is our passion for books that inspires our shared belief that, as the saying goes, there is a book for every child and a child for every book. We believe in the impact that books can make in the lives of readers, and we look for ways to communicate that belief throughout our teaching day. We talk about books with our students whenever we can—when students come in off the bus, during our workshop

Go online to view a video on Reading Workshop in Action. See page 160 for details.

time, even when we see them outside of school. We talk about what we are reading, and we ask students what they are reading. If they don't have a book, we are always ready with a recommendation. During workshop time, we introduce students to many favorite authors and titles. Students also learn how to recommend their own favorites to their peers, just as real, lifelong readers do. We want our students to know that the more they read, the better readers they'll become. In this chapter, we'll review the conditions and components that will elevate your reading workshop and help your students understand the power of books in their lives.

Workshop Conditions

During the summer months, Brian enjoys doing a project (or two) around the house. A few years ago, he constructed a beautiful brick patio on the back of our home using bricks from his family's grocery store (more about those special bricks later). It was a project that took a lot of time and effort, but when it was completed it became the setting for special memories we have shared with family and friends. As we reflect on his work on our patio, we think about the work that we do in our classrooms as we create a space for our reading community. Several important conditions need to be met for this space to be created. It doesn't just happen. It happens deliberately, with a great deal of planning, hard work, and yes, some sweat! A successful workshop includes the following conditions:

- Time
- Materials
- Choice
- Structure
- Mentor or Expert Support

Together, these conditions support our learners in becoming the independent, proficient, and motivated readers that we want them to be, readers who choose to read in their daily lives both within and beyond the walls of the classroom.

We will explore each of these conditions in the workshop setting and give you tips on how they look in our classrooms. We'll help you see how they already exist in your classroom, and give you some suggestions for how to make the most of each component for your readers.

Time

When Brian was working on the patio, he needed time. Uninterrupted time, every day. Sometimes that was frustrating, because it kept him from doing other things that Karen thought were more important than working on the patio. But he was firm in his commitment to his goal, and he devoted time to it each and every day. When he was *finally* finished, Karen understood why he needed the time—and was thrilled with the final product. It was worth it in the end!

The same lesson applies to our readers. They need time and they need it every day. They need time to practice and develop their skills as readers. They also need the time to become engaged with the books that they are reading. That's why one of the most important parts of the workshop is time for students to learn and then apply the skills that they learn through read-alouds and mini-lessons to their independent reading. For your struggling readers, regular reading time allows them to build their reading stamina and confidence.

Below, you will see a sample reading workshop schedule showing one way that you might schedule a 60- or 90-minute block of time in your instructional day, incorporating the different instructional components that make up a reading workshop. Remember that each component is important to your readers. It may be tempting at times to skip one, but devoting time to each component is essential—especially independent reading time. Just as it did with Brian and his commitment to working on the patio each and every day during the summer, staying committed to the schedule will pay off with a beautiful product in the end!

Sample 3–5 Reading Workshop Schedule
(60–90 minutes)

"STATUS OF THE CLASS" (5 minutes)

This quick "check in" may be done at the beginning of reading workshop or at the beginning of the school day. Find out what the student is reading and his or her plan for the day's workshop time. You'll find a reproducible "Status of the Class" form in the online resources.

AND

READ-ALOUD/BOOK TALK (10–15 minutes)

We can introduce students to a wide variety of quality literature through read-alouds (which can often be done at or above their independent/instructional reading level), or through book talks. You'll read more about these teaching routines in Chapter 4.

OR

MINI-LESSON (10–15 minutes)

Teach skills you've identified based on student need or teacher necessity (through the standards or district curriculum) in brief mini-lessons. The mini-lesson may be based on a picture book, a section of a novel, an informational text, or digital media. Clearly identify the purpose of the mini-lesson at the beginning and reinforce it at the end of the lesson. Encourage students to practice the skill during the remaining workshop time.

AND

INDEPENDENT READING / INDIVIDUAL READING CONFERENCES / GUIDED READING
(30–45 minutes)

Students read independently for a sustained period each day to build their stamina and develop reading skills. During this time, the teacher confers with individual readers, getting information about each student that will help guide future instruction. The teacher may also meet with small groups of students with similar reading needs and provide focused reading instruction.

AND

SHARING AND REFLECTION (5 minutes)

To close the workshop, students share something about their reading, such as a favorite part or a strategy they used effectively. This sharing, which takes place either with a partner or the entire class, is a great way to recognize the strides students are making. Another great way to celebrate their progress is to make your students aware of what they did as readers during the workshop time. Ask them, "What did you do well as a reader during workshop time today?" Celebrate their answers and their growth as readers as they progress through the year!

Materials

We mentioned earlier that the bricks Brian used to build our patio were special. They came from the grocery store that Brian's grandparents, then his parents, had owned. Eventually they sold the store, and when it was torn down, Brian and our son Jason collected the bricks from the rubble, stacked them, and transported them the 30 miles to our home. Using those bricks in the patio made it special.

Materials help make our classrooms special, too, both to us and to our students. Exciting books motivate students to read. But not every student will find the same books exciting. Given the range of reading abilities and interests in a typical classroom, it is essential that you provide your readers with access to as many books as possible.

Ideally, your classroom library should have at least 10–15 books per child for your readers to be successful in reading workshop (Atwell, 2007). The books should represent a range of topics, genres, levels, and reading abilities to ensure that each child is able to find a book at his or level that is of interest. We know that sounds like a lofty goal, but it can be an important one for readers to be successful, not only during their time within your classroom but for the rest of their reading lives. Maintaining a classroom library isn't easy for teachers, who often have to do so out of their own funds. Here are some ways to keep your classroom library well stocked with quality literature:

- **Be a reader yourself.** Know books that you can recommend for your readers. You are your students' first resource!

- **Borrow books from your school and public library.** Many public libraries will gather books for you on topics related to areas of study and will have them waiting for you to pick up! They may even let you check out more books for longer periods of time than other patrons because you are a teacher.

Provide students time daily to practice and develop their skills as readers.

Tips for Sharing About Your Reading

※ Tell about a favorite part or a part that surprised you in your reading.

※ Tell whether you would recommend this book to others, and why.

※ Share a strategy that helped you as a reader.

※ Identify vivid vocabulary or figurative language in your book.

Provide a wide range of independent reading material to meet students' interests and range of reading levels.

Build a community of readers where they begin to recommend books to each other based on their interests.

Other Ways to Match Readers With Books

❋ Favorite authors

❋ Series books

❋ Genre titles

❋ Interests

❋ Recommendations from other readers

- **Build your classroom library from book clubs.** Scholastic (our favorite!) is a great resource for inexpensive quality literature, and you can use bonus points. Book clubs are a great way to expose parents to quality children's books. Parents often ask us to recommend good books for their children to read that are at grade level and appropriate. We give them the book flyers. Even if they don't order, the flyers are great resources to take to the public library to help with book selection.

- **Shop garage sales and thrift shops.** When teachers retire or no longer need their collections, they often donate their books. Frequently, if you let sellers know that you are a teacher, they will give you a discount, or even donate unsold books to your classroom.

- **Invite students to donate a book to your classroom library as a fun way to celebrate birthdays and holidays.** Think of it: if 25 students each donate a book to your classroom library, you'll have 25 new (or gently used) books by the end of the year. Create a special bookplate that the students call fill out when they donate the book. Siblings will enjoy looking for the book that an older brother or sister donated and reading it during reading workshop time!

As you add to your classroom library, always take a moment to share new titles with the class or with an individual reader. Often these new additions quickly make the rounds among groups of students because of an enthusiastic introduction. When this happens, you know that book has *really* hooked your readers.

Choice

Our students appreciate and are motivated by the choices that we give them in reading workshop. Often, choice is the missing piece for our reluctant readers. We know that if students have something that genuinely interests them, they can often read a more challenging text because they are motivated to read it.

"Know your reader" is one of the most important things we do in our reading workshop as we look to match students with books. A favorite interest survey of ours, from the *Next Step Guided Reading Assessment* (Richardson & Walther, 2013), keys in on students' overall interests by simply asking them to identify topics they like. This grade-specific survey can serve as the basis for a first reading conference where we begin to match readers with text.

Structure

We've been doing a lot of reading and thinking about the ideas of P. David Pearson (2011), specifically the gradual release of responsibility. Pearson outlines a methodology in which teachers begin by giving students support until they are ready to work independently, then removing support and letting them work on their own. If we see that they are not quite ready or if they need our support again, we bring them back and teach some more, then release them again. We think of it as teach, release, teach, release . . . as needed. The key is to recognize when they are being successful in their new learning and when they need our support. What matters most is that the routines we put in place help our students become capable, independent learners. Here are a few tips on structure that have worked for us and our students over the years:

- **Be predictable.** For many students, especially those with special needs, creating a predictable routine is vital to their understanding of what is happening now and what is happening next. This predictability enables them to focus on their learning, free of anxiety. Creating a daily schedule within your workshop also helps you plan your teaching time effectively. Having materials organized and knowing what you need and when you need it helps make good use of the precious instructional minutes that you have with your students.

- **Be flexible.** It may sound like an oxymoron, but it is just as important to be flexible as it is to be predictable in your reading workshop. Teachable moments arise when you least expect them, and you just have to take advantage of them when they do. For instance, when you're doing independent reading, your students are engaged, and they may need a few more minutes with their books. Being flexible with your schedule means being able to make decisions about your time during workshop based on the needs of your students. Remember, you are the one making the decisions about how you are using the time during your workshop, and you want to do what is best for your readers!

- **Be prepared:** Our lessons always go better when we are prepared. Having the basic elements on hand—the mentor text for read-aloud, books for book talking, and chart paper and markers—makes any lesson go more smoothly. It also enables us be present in the moment and not distracted as we frantically search for the materials we need for an activity.

Mentor or Expert Support

A significant body of research exists to support the importance of the teacher in the classroom (Stuhlman & Pianta, 2009). No matter what program or curriculum you follow, none of it matters as much to your students as you do! Remember that you make a difference in the lives of students you teach. You have the power to guide them toward becoming lifelong readers. Being that force for change is a tremendous responsibility, but it is also one of the most rewarding aspects of the teaching profession.

We think of the '80s television comedy series *Cheers* when we think of Brian going to our local Home Depot store, because everyone knows his name. When he is working on a home improvement project, he is there multiple times a day. He goes there not just for supplies and materials but to talk to the experts who can give him guidance on his current project. We teachers are the experts for our students, providing them with the support and guidance they need to move on to increasingly complex texts. The standards themselves say, "Even many students on course for college and career readiness are likely to need scaffolding as they master higher levels of text complexity" (NGA Center and CCSSO, Appendix A, p. 9). As classroom teachers, we provide the scaffolding for students within our reading workshop. As students become more successful, we lessen the amount of scaffolding we offer and encourage them to be independent. With enough time, well-selected materials, empowered student choices, purposeful structure, and you as their guide, your students will be motivated to become the independent readers we want them to be.

Workshop Components

How do we plan for a reading workshop that meets these conditions while also addressing the importance of teacher language and environment discussed in Chapter 1 and the integrated standards-based practices discussed in Chapter 2? We do so by reflecting on both where we are and how we might move forward. In the Transforming Teaching chart below, we've outlined the instructional shifts necessary to elevate your reading workshop.

TRANSFORMING TEACHING

Somewhat random selection of books used for read-alouds, small groups, and individuals.	Intentional selection of books, some organized by text sets and ordered using a ladder of complexity.
Mainly fiction texts with some nonfiction integrated here and there.	Informational texts play a more prominent role.
Two-way conversations (teacher-student, student-student) are most prevalent and occur mostly in reading and writing instruction.	Collaborative conversations initiated by students in response to peers' questions, thoughts, and opinions take place throughout the day.
Reading responses are based on prior knowledge and experiences.	Reading responses are based on prior knowledge and experience coupled with text-based evidence.
Mini-lessons focus on individual strategies and skills from state standards, district curriculum, or packaged program scope and sequence.	A series of mini-lessons centers on big ideas integrated across language arts strands (reading, writing, speaking, listening, viewing/visually representing).
Comprehension strategies are the focus.	Overarching themes and big ideas are the organizing feature. Comprehension strategies serve as tools to better understand text.
Reading conferences have no clear purpose.	Teachers guide students through a variety of reading conferences that help readers set goals and tackle more complex texts. Teachers meet regularly with students based on individual needs.
Everyone, including the teacher, reads during silent reading time if time is allotted for it.	Support independent reading with structures, such as explicit instruction and teacher monitoring, to increase students' accountability and progress toward reading more complex texts.
Sharing is focused on *what* readers did or learned during workshop time.	Sharing is focused on *how* readers processed complex texts during independent reading time.

As we shared in Chapter 2, each component of the reading workshop, when planned with the standards in mind, can be transformed for your students. In this chapter, we will review the foundational pieces of a workshop and share how to elevate each part by making strategic instructional moves. Then, in Part 2, we will share specific teaching routines and inquiry experiences that address various components for each reading standard. As you read through the components in the box on page 39, view them as a menu rather than a checklist. So, for example, although independent reading,

 Transforming Literacy Teaching in the Era of Higher Standards, Grades 3–5 © 2015 by Karen Biggs-Tucker and Brian Tucker, Scholastic Teaching Resources

read aloud/mini-lesson, and sharing should take place every day, the remaining elements may not. Depending on your instructional purpose, you may choose to spend time one day on collaborative conversations or a reader's response to a text. Your professional decision-making based on the needs of your students and your instructional focus is the key to balancing the components of workshop.

Read-Aloud

Many teachers in the intermediate grades think that read-aloud experiences belong only in the primary classroom. If they do read aloud to their students, it is only a chapter or two from a novel when the students come in from recess. We often read books like this for the enjoyment of the story and to build community with our readers. But we also find the read-aloud to be a powerful instructional tool in reading workshop. You can see a summary of its benefits in the box below. When we want to teach a strategy or launch an inquiry experience, a well-selected picture book is often the best way to start. Many quality books engage readers through both the text and the illustrations. Because they contain minimal text, these books can be read in one or two sittings. This allows us to return to them later and view them through another lens in either reading or writing workshop.

Applying comprehension strategies, identifying key ideas and details, exploring craft and structure, building vocabulary and background knowledge—all this and more can be accomplished as you

A Quick Look at the Components of a 3–5 Reading Workshop

* Read-Aloud
* Collaborative Conversations
* Reading Response
* Mini-Lessons
  * Inspiring and Motivating Readers
  * Comprehension Strategies
  * Foundational Skills (Word Recognition and Fluency)
  * Language Standards (Grammar and Vocabulary)
  * Genre/Text Type Awareness
* Guide Readers Through Conferring
* Independent Reading
* Reflecting and Celebrating

Why Read Aloud in Intermediate Classrooms?

Reading aloud during reading workshop has many advantages for your readers, It:

* builds reading community.
* encourages rich whole-class discussion that is especially valuable before students respond to the text in writing.
* models the teacher's thought process, fluency, and expression, as well as how experienced readers apply strategies, monitor comprehension, and are metacognitive about their reading.
* exposes readers to a range of complex texts, providing opportunities to compare and contrast literary texts and informational texts.
* demonstrates how authors use illustrations and texts to create meaning in a variety of text types.
* enriches vocabulary through a wide range of texts and genres, and by fostering conversations with others.

Source: Adapted from Month-by-Month Reading Instruction for the Differentiated Classroom *(Walther & Phillips, 2012)*

read aloud quality texts and model the behaviors and strategies of experienced readers. The next step is releasing responsibility to students. In read-alouds we do this by fostering conversations in which students share their thinking in pairs, small groups, or with the whole group. In this way, students can practice using strategies and thinking through complex texts with support. Such oral rehearsal leads students to apply these skills independently during individual reading time or when writing a reading response. You'll find more on collaborative conversations on page 43.

Read-aloud is also a time to introduce texts that might be too challenging or complex for students to read independently, because of a new structure, challenging content, or unfamiliar vocabulary. Think aloud as you read aloud, allowing students opportunities to respond and discuss their thinking throughout the process. After you have read all or part of the text together, invite students to read it on their own, either independently or with a partner.

Our Favorite Books About the Power of Reading

Title, Author	Brief Summary
The Fantastic Flying Books of Mr. Morris Lessmore (Joyce, 2012)	Mr. Lessmore finds happiness in a magical library where he cares for books, and ultimately the books care for him.
Open This Little Book (Klausmeier, 2013)	Stories told through many books lead the reader on an adventure about the magic of books.
Book (Lyon, 1999)	A story of the wonders of books and reading, told from the perspective of readers.
Thank You, Mr. Falker (Polacco, 1998)	Trisha's grandfather has told her about the joy of reading, but Trisha still struggles with books until she meets Mr. Falker. He helps unlock the magic of reading and identifies her undiagnosed learning problem.
My Pet Book (Staake, 2014)	A boy and his pet book go everywhere together until the day his faithful companion is lost. Will these friends be reunited?

CREATING TEXT SETS

Develop Text Sets → *Intentional selection of books, some organized by text sets and ordered using a ladder of complexity.*

During the school day, we read books aloud for different purposes. We might read a text in reading workshop for enjoyment or to focus on comprehension strategy and later read the same text in science, focusing on a particular topic. Text sets—literary texts or a combination of literary and informational texts built around a topic or theme—have proven to be a particularly effective means of streamlining our planning and managing our time throughout the instructional day.

Creating an effective text set requires purposeful and strategic planning. You probably have lots of books, but you may not be sure how to combine them into a text set to use with your students. Follow

MULTI-GENRE TEXT SET—STARS

Poem: "The Star" by Jane Taylor, found in *The Bill Martin Jr Big Book of Poetry* (Martin, Jr., 2008, p. 44)

Picture Book: *Stars* (Ray, 2011)

Informational Book: *Stars* (Simon, 2006)

MULTI-GENRE TEXT SET—ABRAHAM LINCOLN

Poem: "Abraham Lincoln" found in *Rutherford B., Who Was He? Poems About Our Presidents* (Singer, 2013, p. 14)

Picture Book: *Just in Time, Abraham Lincoln* (Polacco, 2011)

Informational Book: *Looking at Lincoln* (Kalman, 2012)

MULTI-GENRE TEXT SET—WOLVES

Poem: "The Wolf," found in *The Bill Martin Jr. Big Book of Poetry* (Martin, Jr., 2008, p. 18)

Picture Book: *Wolf!* (Bloom, 1999)

Informational Text: *Wolves* (Simon, 2009)

Steps to Creating a Multi-Genre Text Set

1. Identify a content-area topic or literary theme to base a text set on.

2. Determine types of texts you'd like in your text set (e.g., fictional, informational, poetry, digital), based on your instructional purposes or the interests of your students.

3. If applicable, identify reading level or a range of reading levels for the selected texts.

4. Find engaging texts that support your topic and purpose, and that fall within your target reading-level range(s).

---

the steps in the box above to create text sets to meet your instructional goals. We use two types of text sets in our classrooms: multi-genre and multi-level.

Multi-Genre Text Set

Multi-genre text sets help readers in several ways. They get students talking about subjects that are both literary and informational and helps them integrate knowledge and ideas. Text sets specifically address the reading standard that expects students to "analyze how two or more texts address similar themes or topics in order to build knowledge or to compare the approaches the authors take." (NGA Center and CCSS, p. 10) A few multi-genre text sets to get you started are shown above.

Multi-genre text sets will not only help you achieve the learning demanded by higher standards, they will also build students' background knowledge about a variety of topics. You will also continue to help your students develop the skills and strategies needed to read increasingly complex texts.

Multi-Level Text Sets

Multi-level text sets help readers comprehend increasingly complex text. This is especially important to readers who are struggling or who appear to be stagnant in their reading growth. Creating a text set that explicitly moves the reader into more challenging texts, and builds confidence along the way, is just one way to develop independence in your readers.

To create a multi-level text set, choose three to five texts of genuine interest to your students. Read each one, then order them by complexity. You might want to think about including a variety of texts, such as a mix of fiction and informational books. As you're ordering your texts, consider the following characteristics:

Using Multi-Level Text Sets to Move Reading to More Complex Text

If you have a student who is reading . . .
Timmy Failure: Mistakes Were Made (Pastis, 2013)

. . . move to a more complex title, such as . . .
My Life as a Book (Tashjian, 2010) or *The Strange Case of Origami Yoda* (Angleberger, 2010)

If you have a student who is reading . . .
The Dork Diaries: Tales From a Not So Fabulous Life (Russell, 2009)

. . . move to a more complex title, such as . . .
11 Birthdays (Mass, 2010) or *A Tangle of Knots* (Graff, 2013)

- *Vocabulary*—Think about the vocabulary in the books that you have chosen. Does the vocabulary challenge your reader or will it be too frustrating? Will readers be able to use contextual clues to figure out the meaning of unknown words?

- *Content*—As you read the books aloud, note the themes and concepts being presented. The content of some books may be more appropriate for more mature readers, so be sensitive to your readers' level of sophistication. Select books that challenge them but are sensitive to their emotional development as well.

- *Length*—Reluctant readers are often drawn to short books, yet we want them to move toward longer, more complex texts. Think about how and when to help struggling readers take this important step. Readers must develop the necessary stamina and confidence before attempting longer, more complex texts or their comprehension will suffer.

Once you have created multi-level text sets, you have the opportunity to include your readers in the planning of their own reading growth; see pages 49, and 71–72. As students gain confidence, they will begin to choose more challenging books on their own.

INCORPORATE INFORMATIONAL TEXTS

Incorporate Informational Texts ⟶ *Informational texts play a more prominent role.*

As we read the new standards, we recognize the need for more informational text in our classrooms. Like you, we already have too much to do in our overscheduled days, but this change can be an easy one. We always look for ways to pair a fiction title with a nonfiction title in our read-aloud experiences. These purposeful read-aloud pairings enable us to create a natural balance for our students.

Using informational texts in reading workshop is a proven way to develop your students' background knowledge, whether through a read-aloud, independent reading, or a collaboration with peers. These texts also provide teachers with opportunities to discuss how and where to find information and how to access a variety of resources to learn about topics.

Wonderopolis is another of our favorite ways of getting students reading, writing, and talking about informational text. This website posts a new article daily on a variety of topics, making it a great resource for shared-reading or independent-reading materials. We love to share these pieces with our students every day, and if we forget, they let us hear about it! The articles provide an authentic way to develop background knowledge on a range of topics, and they are easy to incorporate into either reading or writing workshop.

A Few of Our Favorite Informational Read-Alouds

Title, Author	Brief Summary	
On a Beam of Light: A Story of Albert Einstein (Berne, 2013)	Even as a young boy, Albert was fascinated by questions. His curiosity led him to make some of our greatest scientific discoveries. What questions will our young learners ask, and what future discoveries will they make?	
How They Choked: Failures, Flops, and Flaws of the Awfully Famous (Bragg, 2014)	A collection of stories of famous mistakes, some of which turned into surprising successes. Includes stories about the Titanic, Marco Polo, Thomas Edison, and Amelia Earhart.	
Carnivores (Reynolds, 2013)	The lion, the wolf, and the shark feel misunderstood. They want to prove to the plant eaters in the jungle that they just can't help what they do, but trying to become more likeable proves to be quite a challenge.	
JFK (Winter, 2013)	When John F. Kennedy was a young boy, he resolved to change the world. He made good on his vow when he became the 35th president of the United States.	

Collaborative Conversations

> **Collaborative Conversations** → *Collaborative conversations initiated by students in response to peers' questions, thoughts, and opinions take place throughout the day.*

Our reading workshop time is filled with lots of talk—teacher to student, student to teacher, and lots of discussion between students. We confess that it hasn't always been this way. Our workshop has evolved as we have learned how important it is for students to talk about their learning and their thinking. In addition, we have realized over the years that talk is one of the most underutilized instructional tools in our classrooms. As teachers, we spend so much time trying to get our students to be quiet that we sometimes forget just how valuable it is for them to talk to one another. As we tell our students, "You are all experts and can learn as much from each other as you can from us."

As we began to look at what we needed to do to meet the higher standards, it occurred to us that having our students think aloud together would greatly benefit them in their test preparation. In Chapter 6, there are two inquiry experiences that will guide you in supporting students as they learn to pose questions and collaborate. The standards themselves say that students need to be "more adept at drawing evidence from the text and explaining that orally and in writing" (Coleman & Pimentel, 2012, p. 27).

The speaking and listening standards are organized into the following two strands:

- Comprehension and Collaboration
- Presentation of Knowledge and Ideas

Foster a place where students can converse with each other productively.

The standards clustered under the first strand are the ones that you focus on during your read-aloud experiences. These whole-class comprehension conversations help prepare your readers for your reading conference conversations as well as for written responses to reading. They are essential in developing the habits of mind discussed in Chapter 2.

Our students will need to support their thinking and communicate it to others. Providing opportunities for them to practice those skills daily is one way that we give students confidence in their abilities. We have many turn-and-talk times throughout our day, but we think that our students benefit the most from the conversations that happen during our read-aloud times. This talk allows them to process their comprehension thinking with another reader. From asking questions to making predictions, they are able to think (and talk about) how they understand text, especially the more complex texts that we share during read-aloud time. In doing so, they learn to do what the standards ask of them. The conversation becomes a ladder that they ascend to higher-level thinking. Students need modeling and opportunities to practice skills before they are able to participate in these quality conversations independently. Our experience tells us that these conversations do not occur without careful planning. Creating a classroom environment of respect on the first day of school goes a long way in fostering a place where students can converse productively. Additionally, giving students questions to guide their conversations (see box on p. 45) helps get them started until they are able to generate their own conversations independently.

Reading Response

> **Reading Response** → *Reading responses are based on prior knowledge and experience coupled with text-based evidence.*

After students have had opportunities to discuss their thinking among themselves and with the teacher, they are better prepared to write about their reading. While research supports the idea that readers who write about their reading show an increased level of comprehension (Literacy Implementation Guidance for the ELA Common Core State Standards, IRA, 2012, p. 3), this can be a challenging skill to acquire and a difficult skill to teach.

A wonderful way for students to practice writing about their reading is by creating a reader's notebook, where they can collect lessons drawn from whole-class reading discussions and write down their own reactions to their reading; see suggestions in the box on page 45.

Ideas for Reader's Notebook Responses

Students may

✳ write a book review.

✳ write about how they used a reading strategy.

✳ write a character sketch.

✳ write a letter to a friend about why he or she would like a particular book.

✳ draw a comic strip of a favorite part of a book.

✳ write an alternate ending to a book.

✳ compare and contrast a current book to one they've read previously.

✳ write something they've learned about themselves as a reader.

Provide readers time to write about their reading for increased levels of comprehension.

We have limited space in our rooms for anchor charts, and our experience tells us that our older students aren't as dependent on visual material as younger students are. Yet we do believe in creating anchor charts together to capture the thinking of the group. Sometimes we ask students to copy an anchor chart in their notebooks, or we type up the chart later and have students glue it in their reader's notebooks at the beginning of the next day's reading workshop. Students do refer back to the anchor charts in their notebooks when they are creating written responses to their reading. We also hope that they will continue to use their notebooks at home or as they move on in their schooling.

Mini-Lessons

> **Mini-Lessons →** *A series of mini-lessons centers on big ideas integrated across language arts strands (reading, writing, speaking, listening, viewing/visually representing).*

Mini-lessons are an integral part of our reading workshop. They usually focus on the following aspects of reading:

- Inspiring and Motivating Readers
- Comprehension Strategies
- Foundational Skills (Word Recognition and Fluency)
- Language Standards (Grammar and Vocabulary)
- Genre/Text Type Awareness

Questions to Guide Students' Collaborative Conversations

✳ What do you think? Why do you think that?

✳ Tell me more about your thinking. Can you explain your thinking?

✳ What did you notice?

✳ How do you know this?

✳ Can you tell me more?

✳ I have the same thinking because . . .

✳ My thinking is different because . . .

✳ I wonder why . . . ?

✳ What else can you say about that?

✳ What do you think? How do you know?

✳ What questions do you still have?

✳ Show me in the text where it supports your thinking.

Sample Mini-Lesson Series

End Goal/Big Idea: Compare and contrast texts in the same genre on their approaches to similar themes.

Preparation	Mini-Lesson 1	Mini-Lesson 2	Mini-Lesson 3	Mini-Lesson 4	Mini-Lesson 5
Carefully select text sets that demonstrate similar and diverse approaches to an easily identifiable theme (e.g., *friendship, bullying*).	Introduce the topic and review the vocabulary of compare/contrast and theme. Share, discuss, and chart observations from first text.	Share, discuss, and chart observations from second text.	Discuss the similarities and differences between the two texts. Discuss why the authors approached the theme in the same/different ways in the two texts.	Invite students to create a written response comparing/contrasting the themes in the two texts. Remind them to include evidence from the texts to support their thinking.	Students may share their responses with a partner or in a small group. Celebrate thinking and learning about text. Encourage students to continue thinking about how different authors approach theme in their independent reading.

· ·

You will find standards-based inquiry experiences that match each aspect of reading in Chapters 6 and 7. A way to transform instruction is to consider the big idea that you want your students to grasp or the skill you want them to use. Then plan your mini-lessons to teach the incremental skills, strategies, and habits of mind to get there, while connecting each one to the larger idea it supports.

COMPREHENSION STRATEGIES

Comprehension Strategies → *Overarching themes and big ideas are the organizing feature. Comprehension strategies serve as tools to better understand text.*

One of the biggest "a-ha" moments we had as we looked at the standards was when we recognized the need to help our readers think about comprehension strategies. We realized that as our students move up the ladder of text complexity, they will need to rely more and more on their reading strategies to "fix up" problems in comprehension (Pearson, 2011). We knew that this would be especially true as students encountered more informational text with more complex structures and vocabulary. This realization helped us rethink how we were teaching reading strategies to our students.

We knew that many students came to us with an understanding of reading strategies, but we noticed they only applied them in isolation and did not always recognize when a particular strategy would be most appropriate to use. Our goal was to teach reading strategies that students would actually make use of, like tools in a reading toolbox ready to use when needed.

Introducing students to the Reading Toolbox idea (see online resources, page 160) enables you to review the strategies as well as to clarify the purpose of each strategy, review its uses within fiction and nonfiction, and discuss how it can be helpful in problem-solving text. After reviewing each strategy, we discussed how an experienced reading craftsman knows how to choose the right tool for the job. For example, if you want to hang a picture, a hammer will do the job, not a buzzsaw! The same is true for reading strategies. Sometimes making a connection will help the reader move forward in the text, when summarizing will not. Sometimes, with a complex text, readers may use several strategies together to help discern its meaning. A reading craftsman must be able to pick the right reading-strategy tool for the job.

After thinking aloud about both fiction and informational text, using appropriate reading strategies to help "fix up" our understandings, we have students do some independent practice. We ask them to look for examples in their own reading when they need to use a strategy to help them make meaning of challenging text, and we invite them to share in pairs or small groups. Sharing their thinking together can spark great conversation, and listening to their thinking helps us plan for future instruction.

FOUNDATIONAL SKILLS (WORD RECOGNITION AND FLUENCY)

Foundational skills form the basis of our reading, writing, listening, and speaking skills, yet intermediate teachers we've spoken to are often unclear as to the role of foundational skills in their classrooms. We understand this sentiment, but all of us have readers who need additional support in mastering some of these basic skills. What's more, older readers who need additional support with phonics, word recognition, and fluency benefit greatly from having authentic experiences with foundational skills incorporated into reading workshop; you'll find teaching routines for fluency and word-solving in Chapter 5.

The standards document itself states, "Instruction [in foundational skills] should be differentiated: good readers will need much less practice with these concepts than struggling readers will. The point is to teach students what they need to learn and know what they already know—to discern when particular children or activities warrant more or less attention" (NGA Center and CCSSO, 2010, p. 15). This passage reminds us of the importance of knowing our students and knowing what they need. Reading workshop enables teachers to do just that. Through well-planned lessons, observations, and conferences, teachers gain valuable knowledge as to which students need more support in foundational skills and which ones do not.

Embedding instruction of foundational skills in authentic contexts is also vital. It is often tempting to teach phonics, word recognition, and fluency in isolation, because it seems easier, but in our many years of experience we have learned that this doesn't lead to lasting learning for our students, especially our struggling and reluctant readers. The International Reading Association also confirms this notion, advising us that "instruction in Foundational Skills should occur in concert with instruction related to Reading, Writing, Speaking and Listening, and Language" (Literacy Implementation Guidance for the ELA Common Core State Standards, IRA, 2012, p. 2). Providing instruction within a context always helps students know the "what" and the "why" of their learning. We tell our readers that reading fluently helps give reading a flow, and that flow helps comprehension and understanding of the text. Giving students a purpose for reading fluently can motivate them to practice in order to become more fluent readers.

LANGUAGE STANDARDS (GRAMMAR AND VOCABULARY)

The language standards are organized under these three bands:

- **Conventions of Standard English:** Instruction in grammar and usage in both written and spoken language, including spelling instruction

- **Knowledge of Language:** Instruction in formal and informal written/spoken language

- **Vocabulary Acquisition and Use:** Instruction in determining the meaning of words, understanding the relationship between words/word nuances, and using learned words/phrases

This organization helps us see where in our instructional day we should focus on these skills and strategies. Obviously, teaching your students the conventions of standard English and spelling will take place mostly in writing workshop and during word study lessons so students have immediate opportunities to apply their learning. Effective vocabulary instruction is woven into both workshops.

The value of vocabulary and its development is well documented. Students with well-developed vocabularies are not only successful readers and writers, they are also higher-achieving students (Beck, McKeown, & Kucan, 2013).

Within the standards, under the strand "Vocabulary Acquisition and Use" students are asked to "determine or clarify the meaning of unknown words" and "demonstrate understanding of figurative language, word relationships and word meanings (p. 29)." It is important that we recognize the connectedness of this strand with Reading Anchor Standard 4: "Determine the meaning of words and phrases used in a text." We can take a single text, such as a read-aloud or a student's independent reading book, and teach to both language standards and reading standards within the same learning experience. Students may then independently practice the skill in their self-selected independent reading book or another piece of text you provided. "Research shows that the explicit teaching of the meanings of such words and parts of words, along with reading to students and encouraging them to engage in their own extensive reading, can steadily build such vocabulary knowledge" (IRA CCSS Committee, 2012, p. 3). This underscores the vital importance of both read-aloud and independent reading routines during reading workshop. We can connect our instruction and teach multiple standards through individual learning experiences, making our teaching more efficient and effective at the same time.

Guide Readers Through Conferring

> **Conferring** → *Teachers guide students through a variety of reading conferences that help readers set goals and tackle more complex texts. Teachers meet regularly with students based on individual needs.*

Conferring with readers is one of our favorite, and most productive, times during reading workshop. It is a time when we get to sit down one-on-one with each of our students, see where they are and what they need, and then help them create a plan to move forward. We'll admit it isn't always easy, and we are still refining how to manage these conferences within our ever-changing days, but we do believe that it's well worth the effort!

As our practice of conferring with our students has evolved over the years, we have learned that it is important to meet with our students as often as possible. But how to do that, with all the assemblies, fire drills, and the unexpected "show and tell" that we just couldn't resist? We finally gave ourselves permission to do as much as we can, as often as we can, and see as many of our students as time allows each week. Some students we see every day if they need it, and other students we see only once a week. If it's an especially busy week at school, we adjust our expectations of ourselves (just as we would adjust our expectations of our students) and create a new plan of action.

In our conferring practice, we have found it helpful to create clear

Confer with students to provide instruction on comprehension and word-solving strategies, as well as to help them move up the ladder of text complexity.

parameters. We have a set purpose in mind when we meet with each student, and this helps both of us know what to expect during our time together.

TYPES OF READING CONFERENCES

Assessing

Whether we are checking a student's word-recognition skills and comprehension through an informal reading inventory or learning about his or her reading attitudes through a survey, conferences help us collect data that informs our instruction. When our students read to us from a self-selected book or tell us about their at-home reading habits, we gain valuable information about them. We might use that information to help us choose a new, "just right" book, set a new reading goal, or identify a topic for an upcoming mini-lesson.

Teaching

Teaching conferences allow us to follow up on information gleaned from an assessment conference or observations made during whole-class instruction. The student will often leave the teaching conference with something to practice in independent reading that will move him or her forward in reading development until the next time we meet.

Goal Setting

One of the most important things we do in our workshop is to give students responsibility for their own learning. In a goal-setting conference, we invite the student to select a reading objective he or she is determined to meet. The goals may be related to the student's reading habits, a skill or strategy, or another aspect of his or her reading development. Once a goal is chosen, we work together to identify steps to meet the goal, perhaps with the student identifying how the teacher and others might be helpful. We agree on additional times to meet and monitor the progress being made toward the goal, adjusting it as necessary. (See sample goal setting forms on p. 72 and in the online resources, page 160.)

Sharing

As we thought about the different types of purposes of our one-on-one meetings, we realized how important it is to include a conference for us and our readers to simply get together to share about books. This may be an opportunity to share a new title or genre a student has chosen or to discuss an author in a one-to-one setting. Having conversations with our readers about the books they're reading provides a model of what we want them to do when they leave our classrooms. It shows our students how to talk with their peers about what they're reading. This is another way that the collaborative conversations we build into workshop time leak out of workshop and permeate the lunchroom, the playground, and beyond.

Independent Reading

Independent Reading → *Support independent reading with structures, such as explicit instruction and teacher monitoring, to increase students' accountability and progress toward reading more complex texts.*

Research confirms that the more one reads, the better reader one becomes (Krashen, 2004). But to become a proficient reader, a student needs to be motivated to read, not only at school but also at home. Reading self-selected books in reading workshop helps build stamina, motivation, and the reading identities of your students. These may not be terms that are specifically addressed in the standards, but we know that they will lead our readers to read increasingly complex texts and become lifelong readers.

Independent reading time is a proven means of achieving those over-arching goals. Yes, simply allowing our students time to read, and to practice the strategies learned in whole-group instruction or reinforced in a reading conference, sends the important message that reading matters and is something that should be done every day.

How We Support Readers During Independent Reading

STATUS OF THE CLASS

Every reading workshop begins when our readers "check in" with the title and author of the book they are reading and the page number they are on in the book. We record this information on our Status of the Class form. This gives us an easy way to see where everyone is at the beginning of reading workshop.

DRIVE-THRU CONFERENCES

Sometimes we'll do what we like to call drive-thru conferences. These are quick conversations—one or two minutes—where we might help a reader find a new book or review a strategy prior to independent reading time. A quick glance at the Status of the Class sheet can tell us a lot about our readers and point us toward the ones who might need a little help . . . and sometimes a little help can go a long way!

READING LOG

Having students record the books they have finished reading on a "Books I've Read" reading log gives us valuable insight into their reading patterns, such as, *Are they reading a particular author or genre? Do they need help selecting books that are more challenging? Are they abandoning books rather than finishing them?* This becomes an important tool as we meet with students and offer them guidance. The reading log also helps students see the patterns in their own reading, as well as keep a tally of the number of books they have read during a semester or year.

Record the title and page for every student at the beginning of reader's workshop.

SOMEDAY LIST

In reading workshop, students develop individual reading plans for what they are going to read next. To aid in reinforcing this valuable habit of lifelong readers, we provide students with a Someday List to list books that they might choose to read someday, or books that we've talked about in class or that others have recommended. Talking about the Someday List during a reading conference is a great conversation starter, one that allows teachers to guide students toward a book that is not only more challenging but also interesting and motivating.

Track and record the titles of books after students finish them.

Use a Someday List to develop a reading plan.

When students select their own books, they are more motivated to read them. Our classrooms are stocked with quality reading materials and we offer guidance in helping readers choose. But ultimately the choice is in their hands. It's true that we read the occasional text set as a small group or a whole class, but our reading workshop is mostly built around student choice.

Sharing and Celebrating

> **Sharing and Celebrating** ⟶ *Sharing is focused on how readers processed complex texts during independent reading time.*

Reading workshop provides students with an opportunity to reflect on their learning and self-assess. Although it is often overlooked in the hustle and bustle of the school day, time for reflection is an important means of empowering your students and giving them a stake in their own learning. Reflection only takes about five minutes at the end of workshop, but it serves a valuable purpose as students take the time to think about themselves as learners.

The new standards ask students to think more critically, so we must allow them the time to be metacognitive—to think about their thinking. As they assess their performance as thinkers during a particular lesson, we can use their insights to plan future lessons that are responsive to our students, both as a whole group and as individuals.

One way of having students self-reflect at the end of reading workshop is for them to talk with a partner or in small groups, with everyone having an opportunity to share. Another way is having them write in their reader's notebook about one thing that they did well as a thinker during workshop and something that they would like to do better next time. If there is time, students might share their ideas with the whole group. We like to stress with students that we are all learning together, so there is no one right answer at any time!

What are some ways that you have students reflect on their thinking in your classroom? How can you use reading workshop as a time to for self-reflection among your students? We bet that you have some great ideas to add to our list!

Schedule time for students to read independently the books that they have self-selected.

Why Independent Reading Is Essential

Independent reading:

❋ builds reading stamina.

❋ cultivates reading identity and individual reading preferences.

❋ develops ability to read increasingly complex text.

❋ provides time to apply and practice reading strategies.

❋ communicates the importance of daily reading.

❋ fosters a lifelong love of reading!

Looking Back, Moving Forward

The core conditions are the same, whether it is building a patio for your family or creating a workshop for your students. Focusing on time, materials, choice, structure, and mentor or expert support helps create an environment that is engaging for students and encourages them to take risks. But can the conditions that work successfully in reading workshop translate into other learning settings? The answer is a resounding YES, and we'll show you how you can take what works well for your learners in reading workshop and smoothly transition that into an effective writing workshop!

Chapter 4

Enhancing Writing Workshop

Teaching Writing in the Real World

We love to teach writing to our students. It is one of the favorite parts of our day. We love to see our writers look forward to writing workshop. We love to see them writing for real reasons, to authentic audiences. Writing workshop is valuable on a practical level, preparing students to meet the high expectations of the standards while generating the enthusiasm for writing that they will need to pursue outside the classroom. That is our ultimate goal as writing teachers.

Go online to view a video on Writing Workshop in Action. See page 160 for details.

Workshop Conditions

Like many teachers, we try to connect our students' efforts as readers to their writing work. However, it took us many years to realize how to use our reading workshop knowledge to strengthen our practices in writing. The increased expectations of the new standards and the ever-changing needs of our students have helped us view our various workshop practices through a new lens. We now see the connections between reading and writing that will ultimately help our students develop the skills they need to be proficient writers—and who write in their daily lives because they enjoy it!

Time

Donald Graves (1994), the father of writing workshop, reminds us that our students need time to write. He recommends that teachers allocate writing time at least four days a week. Writers need that time to think, develop thinking into writing, and craft that writing. Writing workshop is the place for this work to occur.

Provide students with time to write every day.

The National Commission on Writing stresses the importance of developing writing stamina, stating, "If students are to make knowledge their own, they must struggle with the details, wrestle with the facts, and rework raw information and dimly understood concepts into language they can communicate to someone else." In short, "if students are to learn, they must write" (2003, p. 9). Devoting time daily for students to write helps them build writing stamina and understand what real writers do. Teachers often resort to assigning worksheets or other easily managed activities during workshop, but this isn't the real work of writers. Students should be writing, revising, editing, sharing, and publishing their pieces.

The CCSS require that students not only write daily but also write *routinely* and *across disciplines*. This means in writing workshop as well as math, science, and social studies. Writing across the curriculum gives our students opportunities to write a variety of texts for a variety of purposes and audiences.

Writing Routinely for a Variety of Purposes in the Intermediate Classroom

PROVIDE AMPLE TIME TO WRITE

Students of all ages need daily writing practice, but intermediate writers especially need time to develop their ideas into more in-depth pieces.

WRITE ACROSS THE CURRICULUM

Making connections to learning in the content areas is a great way to give students ideas for their daily writing. It also allows them to practice their writing skills and strategies throughout the learning day.

CREATE OPPORTUNITIES FOR AUTHENTIC WRITING FOR A VARIETY OF PURPOSES AND AUDIENCES

Students in intermediate classrooms should have frequent opportunities to see that real writers write for many purposes and for many audiences. Identifying real-life experiences where these skills can be applied helps your readers make these connections in their daily lives.

Sample 3–5 Writing Workshop Schedule

(60–90 minutes)

READING LIKE A WRITER *(10–15 minutes)*

Teachers read and discuss mentor texts related to a particular reading skill with students, then follow up with a conversation and possibly a related writing activity.

OR

MINI-LESSON *(10–15 minutes)*

Brief mini-lessons should be based on a text you've pre-selected, one you've created together with a student, or a piece of student writing. Clarify the purpose for the mini-lesson at the beginning of the lesson, reinforce it at the end, and encourage students to practice the skill during the remaining workshop time.

AND

INDEPENDENT WRITING: INDIVIDUAL WRITING CONFERENCES *(30–45 minutes)*

Students write independently for a sustained period each day to build their stamina. During this time, the teacher conducts writing conferences with individual students, gaining information that will help guide future instruction.

AND

SHARING STUDENT WRITING AND/OR PROCESSING WORKSHOP TIME

(5–10 minutes)

As a closing activity, give students an opportunity to share their writing either with a partner or with the entire class. It's a great way to celebrate their progress as writers. Another way is to provide them with a moment to reflect on their experience by asking, "What did you do well as a writer during workshop time today?" Celebrate their answers and their growth as writers as they progress through the year!

Materials

Writer's notebooks are one of our favorite ways to get our students writing and to develop their writing stamina. These simple tools get students engaged and motivated to write and are an excellent way to start the year and build your writing community. We first became aware of this strategy through one of our favorite writing teachers, Ralph Fletcher. In *A Writer's Notebook: Unlocking the Writer Within You* (1996), Fletcher gives lots of great ideas to get started using notebooks with your students. His book has proved beneficial to students as they begin to understand the nuances of notebook writing. Before introducing the writer's notebook in workshop, we read chapters from Fletcher's book aloud in class and have students partner-read and discuss it together. Students then develop longer writing pieces based on the ideas that they collect in their notebooks.

From teachers, I have heard quotes such as these . . .

"Using writer's notebooks in my classroom has not only changed my teaching, but it has also changed my students as writers. I have always taught my students how to write, but now I am also teaching them the habits of good writers, and our writers' notebooks are the perfect tools to help reinforce each of these lessons. Writer's notebooks have given my students more opportunities to take risks by playing with conventions and different types of writing. Students also use their writers' notebooks as a place to keep their ideas and plan stories. My students feel inspired to write what they are passionate about because they know that they have choice in what is written in their notebooks. As a result I have noticed that my students have truly become writers who find writing and reading important and a part of their everyday lives."
—Noor Shammas, fourth-grade teacher, Oswego, IL

Encourage writers to personalize their writer's notebooks.

IDEAS FOR LAUNCHING THE WRITER'S NOTEBOOK

Personalizing the Notebook

- Decide what type of notebooks students will use for their writer's notebooks. We recommend marble composition books, which are the most durable. Have students bring them in during the first week of school.

- Invite students to decorate their notebooks with pictures brought from home or printed out at school. Pictures and text can represent the interests and hobbies of students. Encourage students to show their unique personalities through the process of personalizing the notebook.

- Have students share their notebooks with partners, in small groups, or with the whole class as a getting-to-know-you activity.

What a Writer's Notebook Is/Isn't

- After reading the introduction to *A Writer's Notebook*, have students create an anchor chart in their writer's notebook titled "What a Writer's Notebook Is/Isn't."

- Have a conversation about the expectations for writer's notebooks in your classroom based on the reading and discussion of Fletcher's book.

- Create a classroom anchor chart with expectations for writer's notebook entries and guidelines. You can keep this chart posted in your room or copy the anchor chart and have students glue it into the notebook to refer to it (or even add ideas) throughout the year.

Why Writer's Notebooks Are Important

A writer's notebook:

- ❋ reinforces the notion that stories are everywhere—at school, at home, anywhere that students have experiences that they can write about.

- ❋ encourages writing beyond the classroom.

- ❋ creates a mind-set that writers practice their craft routinely—not just during writing workshop.

- ❋ encourages students to collect snippets of writing that they may later turn into longer pieces.

- ❋ empowers writers to write frequently throughout the day and throughout the year.

Share Mentor Texts About Writer's Notebooks

- Read aloud books that mention writers' notebooks. Some of our favorites are *Amelia's Notebook* (Moss, 2006), *This Journal Belongs to Ratchet* (Cavanaugh, 2013), *Middle School Is Worse Than Meatloaf* (Holm, 2007), *Born Yesterday* (Solheim, 2010).

- Have students identify characteristics of writer's notebooks based on what they have seen, heard, and read in these or other mentor texts.

- Invite students to look for examples of writers' notebooks in their own independent reading. (You'll be surprised how many authors depict characters writing in notebooks!) Keep a chart in your classroom of some of your favorites.

Watch a Video Showing a Variety of Writers' Notebooks

- Watch the video "A Peek Inside My Writer's Notebook" by Ruth Ayres (YouTube) or any other video related to writers' notebooks. This particular one is our favorite because it shows a variety of writer's notebooks and many different ways that they can be used by writers of any age.

- Create a list of all the different ways that writers use their notebooks. You might need to watch the video several times to see all the ways that it presents, which include creating lists, making maps, drawing pictures of family/friends, and creating word webs.

- Have students identify one or two new ways to use their notebooks as a means of improving their own writing.

Ideas for Writer's Notebook Entries

※ Write about a favorite memory. Describe people, places, and feelings.

※ Tell about something that happened to you or someone you know.

※ Tell about something that you've seen in as much detail as you can.

※ Write about where you would like to go, who would you like to go with, and why.

※ Identify a topic that you consider yourself an expert in. Make a list of everything that you know about your topic.

※ Ask, "What are your 'wonderings'? What might happen if . . . ?"

Create a Heart Map

- Read aloud *My Map Book* (Fanelli, 1995). Discuss the different types of maps and how they are helpful in providing information. Show the "heart map" and discuss how all writers will create one of their own in their writer's notebook to generate ideas for future writing topics.

- Model your own heart map showing the people, places, and things that are important to you. Discuss how these could serve as topics to explore in your writer's notebook.

- Have students create heart maps in their writer's notebooks.

- Encourage them to choose one topic from their heart map to write about in their writer's notebook.

Choice

We know that students are motivated to write (and write more) if they are given the choice of what to write about, yet, as classroom teachers, we struggle with balancing student choice and mandated assignments. We always look for opportunities within those assignments to give students choices. For example, if students need to write an opinion piece for a unit of study, we can allow them to choose their own topic.

In this way, they are fulfilling the expectations of the assignment and showing that they understand the genre, but they are more engaged and motivated to write because they have a choice of topic.

We know that some students have a difficult time coming up with ideas to write about during workshop time. Creating and maintaining a writer's notebook is one way to help students collect ideas that can be transformed into longer pieces, whether they are fiction, informational, or opinion. Getting students started in their notebooks often gives them not only the ideas but also the confidence and the motivation to get started on longer pieces later.

Our favorite way of filling our writer's notebooks with writing ideas is by using mentor texts to start rich conversations about where writers get their ideas for their writing. Some of our favorite mentor texts for helping writers generate ideas are below. Remember that allowing time for writers to listen to, respond to, and then write about great texts is the best way to keep your writers advancing up the literacy ladder.

Writer's Notebook Mentor Texts

Title, Author	Brief Summary
Emily's Blue Period (Daly, 2014)	Emily is an artist who shares her life through her work. When she finds herself going through a rough patch, she creates a beautiful collage heart map that shows the important people in her life.
My Map Book (Fanelli, 1995)	Fanelli presents a collection of a variety of maps, including a heart map.
Amelia's Notebook (Moss, 2006)	Amelia writes about her life in her journal. In words and in doodles that enhance her thoughts, Amelia records friends, family, and what happens at school in her journal pages.
Ish (Reynolds, 2004)	Ramon loves to draw until a careless comment by his older brother makes him question his ability to be an artist. Luckily, he learns a valuable lesson about the value of art from his little sister, Marisol, who creates a "museum" with his work in his room.

Structure

- **Be predictable:** Creating a workshop where the routines serve both you and your students helps set a predictable routine and a congenial atmosphere where good writing can happen and writers can grow. We establish the routines of workshop time (like the workshop schedule on page 54) at the outset of the year, and we adhere to them. Of course, the occasional assembly or fire drill may upset routines, but students know that there will always be a read-aloud or mini-lesson, time for writing, time for conferring, and time for sharing.

- **Be flexible:** Taking an extra moment to talk about a text or giving students a few extra minutes of writing time can be hard to do when we're trying to make every minute count during the school day. But giving our writers some extra time here or there tells them that we truly value their writing and their thinking, and that we value them as writers. Isn't that worth it?

- **Be prepared:** Taking a few minutes at the beginning of the day to gather materials for writing workshop always helps make our time with our students go more smoothly. In addition to their writer's notebooks, students keep rough drafts of their writing in pocket folders so that they can easily access it. Knowing where things are and where they go helps to keep everyone prepared and focused on the task at hand during workshop time.

Mentor or Expert Support

The true mentors of our writing workshop are published authors. First, we identify the authors of the mentor texts that we share in our mini-lesson read-alouds. As we read and examine what they do and how they do it, we begin to see how we can borrow that expertise and try it in our own writing. Some of our favorite authors and mentor texts can be found below.

We also have experts in our own classrooms, whom we recognize when we share student writing samples. We love to look for exemplary student work to share within our workshop. For example, if we are talking about writing great leads, we look at leads from great mentor texts as well as sharing and celebrating those written by our student writers. Doing this not only provides great examples of writing for our students, it also builds their confidence.

A Few of Our Favorite Mentor Texts for Student Writers

Title, Author	Brief Summary
The Plot Chickens (Auch, 2009)	Henrietta loves to read, so she decides to write a book of her own. The story describes the process of writing with a humorous twist—and a nice dose of perseverance!
Ralph Tells a Story (Hanlon, 2012)	Ralph never has anything to write about during writing time. One day his classmates help him realize that his life is full of stories. Then, when he starts writing, he has many stories to share with his class . . . and the world!
Little Red Writing (Holub, 2013)	A clever retelling of "Little Red Riding Hood" in which a little red pencil follows a story path to collect ideas and words for her own story about courage.
This Journal Belongs to Ratchet (Cavanaugh, 2013)	Ratchet is a young girl who is homeschooled and decides to use her journal to write about her life. As she goes through the changes of growing up and learning the truth about her mother, Ratchet uses her notebook and her homeschool writing assignments to better understand herself.

Workshop Components

Providing a predictable time each day for students to write is one of the best ways to help them become the writers we want them to be. It also helps teachers develop a solid routine. Our students look forward to this time each day—in fact, if we ever skip it, they get upset!

Enhancing Writing Workshop

TRANSFORMING TEACHING	
Mentor texts are used to highlight writing techniques.	Mentor texts are used to highlight craft and structure from both the reader's and writer's perspective.
Two-way conversations, with teacher-student being the most common.	Collaborative conversations initiated by students in response to peers' writing, ideas, and suggestions take place throughout the day.
Discrete mini-lessons are based on individual strategies and skills from state standards, district curriculum, or packaged programs.	A series of well-planned mini-lessons centered on big ideas are integrated across language arts strands (reading, writing, speaking, listening, viewing/visually representing).
Spelling is taught as a separate subject or during a separate block.	Spelling strategies are integrated into writing workshop.
Writing strategies or writing traits are the organizing feature of writing workshop.	Overarching themes, big ideas, and genres are the organizing features of writing workshop; qualities of writing or traits are used to strengthen writing.
The study of grammar and conventions occurs outside the writing workshop.	The study of grammar and conventions is integrated into the writing workshop.
Writing genres include narrative, persuasive, and expository.	Writing genres include narrative, opinion, and informational/explanatory; writers learn about different ways to communicate in each genre.
Writers are guided primarily in a whole-class setting.	Independent writing is supported by explicit instruction and teacher monitoring to increase students' accountability and strengthen their writing.
Students write independently while the teacher engages in other activities.	Writers are guided individually based on their specific needs.
Sharing is focused on *what* writers did or learned.	Sharing and celebrating are focused on reflection about *how* writers went about crafting their pieces, the process or strategies that were independently applied.

Establish workshop components that build reading, writing, listening, and speaking connections for your learners.

A Quick Look at the Components of a 3–5 Writing Workshop

❋ Read Like a Writer

❋ Collaborative Conversations

❋ Mini-Lessons

- Words for Writers

- Qualities of Effective Writing

- Writing in Various Forms— Narrative, Expository/ Explanatory, Opinion/ Argument

- Grammar Study

❋ Independent Writing

❋ Conferring With Writers

❋ Sharing and Celebrating

Read Like a Writer

> **Mentor or Expert Support** → *Mentor texts are used to highlight craft and structure from both the reader's and writer's perspective.*

If you love reading aloud to your students as much as we do, you probably also enjoy talking with students about the habits of effective writers. Learning from experienced writers is a great way for students to master important writing skills. The standards focus on the craft and structure of text. Reading like a writer offers us the opportunity to talk about the craft and structure of good writing during writing workshop. As we plan our workshop time, we look for books that include craft techniques such as the following:

- Various text structures

- Sensory language

- Creative conventions

- Onomatopoeia

- Illustration techniques

When we show students how to read from the perspective of an author, it both strengthens their writing skills and aids their comprehension. We show them how the authors craft and structure their texts to help the reader understand the message. In doing so, we also build connections between the reading and writing standards—connections students can then make in their own reading and writing.

Collaborative Conversations

> **Collaborative Conversations** → *Collaborative conversations initiated by students in response to peers' writing, ideas, and suggestions take place throughout the day.*

Students should be involved in a variety of conversations about their writing and the mentor texts read during workshop. Many of your reluctant writers will benefit from a conversation with a teacher or more experienced writer to get them started or keep them writing. Many writers, even at the intermediate level, need to be reminded that writing is talking put on paper. Taking time to choose an idea and verbalize ideas prior to writing or during the writing process boosts the confidence of struggling writers.

Questions to Ask Writers

* What is the best part of your piece? Why?

* What would you change about your piece? Why?

* What did you do differently as a writer in this piece?

* What will you do differently when you write next time?

* What did you learn about yourself as a writer during this process?

The Language of Read-Like-a-Writer Conversations

* What did the author do? Why do you think he or she did that? Would you have done something different? Why?

* How did the author's choices help you understand the text?

* Did the author use any of your favorite words or phrases, or ones you wish you had written?

* Why would an author do something like that? How else could the author have done that?

* Why did the author choose that word? How did it help you understand the text?

(Adapted from Johnston, 2004)

Getting your students engaged in productive conversations about what they read and write requires a significant investment of time and lots of modeling. We like to model with another adult once or twice during the mini-lesson portion of workshop. Then we model a conversation with a student, and finally we have a pair or small group show what a conversation looks and sounds like. All of this modeling helps students see conversations for different purposes taking place. It also prepares students for work they'll be doing on their own and for the writing conferences they will take part in during workshop time.

Mini-Lessons

> **Mini-Lessons** → *A series of mini-lessons centered on big ideas is integrated across language arts strands (reading, writing, listening, speaking, viewing/visually representing).*

In mini-lessons we offer strategically planned lessons that introduce concepts to the whole group and are followed by independent practice. During the writing workshop, mini-lessons are usually focused on the following aspects:

* Words for Writers

* Qualities of Effective Writing

* Grammar Study

* Writing in Various Forms—Narrative, Informative/Explanatory, Opinion/Argument

Plan effective, engaging mini-lessons to teach your students during workshop time.

It can be hard to limit your instruction, but mini-lessons need to be short and sweet. Try to keep them to 10–15 minutes so that students have an opportunity to practice what you have taught them or choose another writing activity to do in their independent writing.

Some Ideas for Keeping Mini-Lessons "Mini"

❋ When reading a mentor text, read a portion of the text or choose a shorter text like a picture book. It's okay to start a picture book one day and finish it the next, as long as that serves the goals of the mini-lesson.

❋ If you will be writing a text with students, write the introductory portion of the text prior to the lesson and write the section that matches your teaching focus during the mini-lesson.

❋ If students are writing a response to a piece, have students create the response one day and share it in small groups the next day.

❋ When students share ideas, have them "turn and talk" with a peer rather than addressing the whole group.

❋ If students are creating an anchor chart, have them write ideas on sticky notes and transfer them to chart paper. Students can review others' ideas during independent writing time.

Sample Mini-Lesson Series

Mini-Lesson 1	Mini-Lesson 2	Mini-Lesson 3	Mini-Lesson 4	Mini-Lesson 5
Introduce the concept. Share and discuss concrete examples using a mentor text or mentor sentences.	Notice and discuss how authors use the concept in their own writing.	Encourage students to practice and apply this concept in other contexts by looking for or creating their own mentor sentence based on the concept.	Invite students to try the concept in their own independent writing.	Share and celebrate student writing.

WORDS FOR WRITERS

Words for Writers ⟶ *Spelling strategies are integrated into writing workshop.*

"Words for Writers" is the time when we focus on words and how they enrich writing. Students are continually adding to their vocabularies and looking to incorporate new words into their writing, but they often hesitate to use these words because they are unsure how to spell them. This often leads them to substitute a less specific or descriptive word. To encourage the use of strong words, we must teach students strategies for spelling longer words and introduce resources they can turn to for help. See our list of strategies on page 63.

Strategies for Supporting Spellers

❋ Encourage students to use vivid vocabulary in their writing even if they are unsure of the spelling of words.

❋ Allow students to continue to use developmental spelling for words that are still challenging for them.

❋ Demonstrate and practice how to spell multisyllabic words by using root words and affixes (including prefixes and suffixes).

❋ Develop word lists of high-frequency words and post them in the classroom or glue them in writer's notebooks for students to reference while writing.

❋ Familiarize students with various spelling and usage resources, e.g., a dictionary, thesaurus, and online resources.

❋ Create a plan for word study instruction and provide for individualized word study as needed.

QUALITIES OF EFFECTIVE WRITING

Qualities of Effective Writing → *Overarching themes, big ideas, and genres are the organizing features of writing workshop; qualities of writing or traits are used to strengthen writing.*

Like you, we determine the content of our mini-lessons based on the needs of our students and the expectations of the standards. As you read the standards, you'll discover that the language of the traits is helpful when discussing the qualities of good writing and can provide a structure for organizing mini-lessons. For example, the introduction to the Common Core writing standards states, "Each year in writing, students should demonstrate increasing sophistication in all aspects of language use from vocabulary [*word choice*] and syntax [*fluency*] to the development [*ideas*] and organization [*organization*] of ideas" (p. 19).

The traits provide common language for teachers and writers to use when discussing writing during workshop time. When you focus your mini-lesson instruction using trait language and use the same language throughout your workshop routines, you will see the language transfer into your students' conversations. Won't it be great when you overhear your learners using terms such as *fluency*, *voice*, and *conventions* as they discuss their writing throughout the day?

The Trait Language of Ideas in the Common Core Standards

❋ Develop and strengthen writing by planning, revising, rewriting (W.3/4/5.5)

❋ Recall relevant information from experiences or gather information from sources (W.3/4/5.8)

❋ Convey ideas and information clearly (W.3/4/5.2)

❋ Develop experiences or events using descriptive details and clear event sequences (W.3/4/5.3)

Revision is an essential habit of successful writers, but in our experience, many intermediate writing students are not especially keen on revising their work. They may be willing to edit it, looking for a few errors, correcting a missing capital letter or punctuation mark, but often they resist the kind of substantial revisions that real writers make. Over the years, we have struggled to find ways to help our students understand the value of revision and help them apply this skill in a manageable way.

In *Write Like This: Teaching Real-World Writing Through Modeling and Mentor Texts* (2011), Kelly Gallagher shares a strategy that we have found to be helpful in getting our writers to become more comfortable with revision. The RADAR strategy ("Replace, Add, Delete, And Reorder") offers a concrete, step-by-step approach to revision for students to use as they reread their writing and look for ways to improve it.

R (Replace)	A (Add)	D (Delete) . . . And	R (Reorder)
• Words that are unclear or overused • Sentences that sound repetitive	• More specific details • Descriptive adjectives or adverbs • Figurative language such as similes and metaphor	• Details that aren't related to your big idea • Repetitive words or phrases	• So that your ideas or details make better sense • So that the flow of your writing continues • So that the details better connect to your main idea

GRAMMAR STUDY

> **Grammar Study** → *The study of grammar and conventions is integrated into the writing workshop.*

The language standards require that students be knowledgeable about the essential rules of standard written and spoken English, but they treat language as a matter of craft and informed choice among alternatives. In Jeff Anderson's book *Mechanically Inclined* (2005), he advocates for the teaching of grammar in authentic, engaging ways. He advises teachers to do the following:

- Teach grammar and convention skills as students need them. Observe their writing and let it tell you when they are ready for a skill. Giving too much instruction at once will overwhelm them and their learning will suffer.

- Immerse students in great models. Mentor texts, your own writing, and student work are all excellent resources you can use to show students what good grammar looks like.

- Post anchor charts in the classroom to review and reinforce skills that you are teaching. Make copies of the charts for students to keep in their writer's notebooks as a reference.

Creating Mentor Sentences

TARGETS

- I can notice and name how conventions are used in mentor texts.

- I can create mentor sentences using conventions correctly.

Transforming Literacy Teaching in the Era of Higher Standards, Grades 3–5 © 2015 by Karen Biggs-Tucker and Brian Tucker, Scholastic Teaching Resources

PREPARATION

Gather a variety of mentor texts that use conventions in a variety of ways. See examples on page 66. It is helpful to have the following materials available for creating mentor sentences:

- Chart paper
- Chalkboard or whiteboard
- Interactive whiteboard
- Sentence strips
- Markers

EXPLANATION

Jeff Anderson (2005) encourages teachers to expose students to sentences that model correct grammar and mechanics usage. For many years, teachers used incorrect models, and asked students to correct sentences with a number of mistakes in them. Having students view model sentences and then respond with sentences of their own instead reinforces the correct usage of conventions and helps students better understand how grammar and mechanics create meaning within a text.

EXPERIENCE

- Identify a mechanics/conventions skill to model with your students (e.g., how commas are used in a sentence, the use of quotation marks in dialogue).

- Select a book or other written piece that demonstrates the skill in question.

- Read the text aloud together, noticing how the author uses the identified skill to help create meaning. See some guiding questions for those conversations on page 66.

- Select one or two sentences to record on chart paper as mentor sentences to demonstrate how the convention is used correctly. Along with the mentor sentence(s), write a rule or two as to how the convention was used in the mentor text.

- Invite students to create their own sentences or look for sentences in their independent reading that demonstrate the convention modeled in the lesson.

- Record sentences on chart paper or on sentence strips and post. Refer back to the rules that were identified, making sure that the convention is staying consistent. If there are exceptions, discuss those and note them on the chart.

- Encourage students to begin incorporating the highlighted skill into their daily writing. Continue to review and reinforce correct usage of the skill in writing workshop mini-lessons.

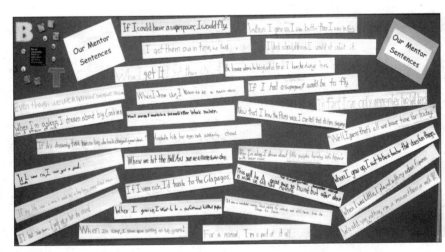

Display students' mentor sentences to reinforce skills taught in mini-lessons.

A Few of Our Favorite Texts Highlighting Conventions

Title, Author	Brief Summary
Punctuation Celebration (Bruno, 2009)	A fun, engaging collection of poems describing punctuation marks and their uses.
Ninja! (Chung, 2014)	A young boy using his ninja skills to achieve a goal is captured and sent to his room. Later he decides to teach the way of the ninja to another young recruit . . . his little sister!
Roller Coaster (Frazee, 2003)	A beautifully written and illustrated narrative about a group of people riding a roller coaster— some of them are veterans, and one is not!
And Then It's Spring (Fogliano, 2012)	The story of a young boy as he "nurses" a young seedling from the cold ground of winter to the warm soil of spring. Will he have the patience to see the first bloom of the new season?

Creating an Editor's Checklist

TARGET

I can edit my writing for correct conventions and grammar.

Questions to Guide a Conventions Conversation

❋ How is the author using this particular convention in his or her writing?

❋ Why do you think he or she chose to use that particular convention? Why do you think he or she chose to use it in that particular way?

❋ How does the convention help you read that sentence aloud?

❋ How does the convention help you read that sentence silently?

❋ How would that sentence sound different if you changed that convention to something else? What would you change and why?

PREPARATION

It is helpful to have the following materials available for students to create their editor's checklists (a sample editor's checklist can be found on page 67):

- Chart paper
- Chalkboard or whiteboard
- Interactive whiteboard
- Markers

EXPLANATION

As students move their written piece through the revising and editing process, we want them to assume the responsibility for editing their own work. Often it can be easier to correct their papers for them in red pen and then just have them make the corrections before creating a final copy, but that doesn't help them learn to apply the skills that we are teaching them. Doing so also creates writers who are dependent on others or who become apathetic about their own writing. The end result is that many students' work is well below grade-level expectations. Ultimately, we want our students to not only attain the literary skills they need to be lifelong readers, but also the motivation to take full ownership of their writing.

EXPERIENCE

- Create a class editor's checklist like the one at right.

- Add important skills you've taught that you expect your writers to have mastered.

- Begin the year with one or two skills and then add the ones you teach in your mini-lessons.

- Copy the list for your students each time an item is added. This becomes their editor's checklist. They can glue it into their writer's notebook or in their writing folder to reference during the editing process.

- Edit the list for individual students as needed. Your special-needs students or reluctant writers may need some extra assistance. Or you can simplify for them by identifying only 1–2 items on their checklist for them to edit.

- Encourage students to refer to the editor's checklist not only during the editing process but also while they are writing individually.

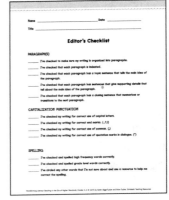

WRITING IN VARIOUS FORMS—NARRATIVE, INFORMATIVE/EXPLANATORY, OPINION/ARGUMENT

> **Developing Genre Forms →** *Writing genres include narrative, opinion, and informational/ explanatory; writers learn about different ways to communicate in each genre.*

Our students are asked to write in a variety of genres to be members of a literate world: lists, narratives, notes, e-mails, blog posts, and so many more. It is hard to imagine that before our students were born, many of us had never heard of a text message or a tweet! We are beginning to recognize that these students will someday be writing in forms that probably have not even been created yet.

To prepare our students for an ever-changing world of literacy, we need to ask them to do a wide range of writing and to remind ourselves that they need to be writing in all the different genres in writing workshop. We also need to help students recognize that writers often include bits of different genres within the same piece. An opinion piece may include a narrative section to connect the reader to the writer before stating the opinion of the text. To help students develop skills in various writing forms, teach mini-lessons that do the following:

- Encourage wide reading of both fiction and nonfiction texts.

- Introduce learners to a variety of genres, both in print and multimedia forms.

- Expose students to digital media and genres found both in and outside of school.

- Discuss how purpose and audience relate to an author's writing.

- Analyze text structures.

- Notice how authors employ various genres within a single piece of text. Discuss how using multiple genres enhances the reader's experience.

- Compare and contrast different genres/text structures.

- Involve students in applying craft structures of genres to their own writing.

Providing our writers with wide exposure to genre forms is like opening up the world to them as writers. Through a variety of texts and many conversations about the choices that authors make when they choose a form in which to write, we familiarize our students with the breadth of options at their fingertips. The next step is guiding them to make their own choices regarding the form their writing will take. Sitting down and having a conversation on this subject is a great place to start.

Critical Classroom Conditions for Effective Independent Writing

❋ *Time*: Daily time in-class to write

❋ *Choice*: Student-selected topics (in additional to teacher-selected topics)

❋ *Effective Mini-lessons*: Purposeful lessons based on both writing skills and the habits of writers

❋ *Opportunities for Goal-Setting*: Goals sets for and by student writers

❋ *Conferring*: Frequent opportunities for conferring throughout the writing process

❋ *Collaborative Conversations*: Frequent opportunities to converse with teacher and peers about writing throughout the process for a variety of purposes to strengthen both the writing and the writer

(Adapted from Fletcher & Portalupi, 2001)

Independent Writing

> **Independent Writing** ⟶ *Independent writing is supported by explicit instruction and teacher monitoring to increase students' accountability and strengthen their writing.*

Students need a frequent, predictable time set aside for them to write daily (Fletcher & Portalupi, 2001), when they can practice and develop the skills presented during mini-lessons. Independent writing time is crucial for student development and should be the largest block of or writing workshop. Graves (1983) reminds us that children want to write, and those who write become better writers. As teachers of writing, we need to allow students writing time on a daily basis.

Independent writing time also allows you a chance to see your mini-lessons in action as students apply them in their daily writing. You can also see what they are transferring successfully and what might need a follow-up reminder or two at the start of tomorrow's mini-lesson. This time also allows you to see a few students who might need some teacher modeling or guided practice in a small group, and it is the perfect time to take a moment or two and pull them together to do this. It is also provides a chance for you, as the teacher, to take a moment, sit back, and observe your learners doing the work of writers. As you look around, observe what your students are doing, notice who is engaged, and who might need some guidance from you during a conference.

Conferring with Writers

> **Guided Writers** ⟶ *Writers are guided individually based on their specific needs.*

Engage in a variety of conferences with your students to help them grow as writers.

An important part of our writing workshop involves giving feedback to our writers. We are constantly looking for effective ways to tell our students what they are doing well in their writing and to help them set goals for what they can do better next time. We also incorporate goal setting into our workshop time, so students look at their own writing and decide what they want to work on improving in the future.

Just as with reading conferences, a writing conference needs a clear purpose. We have created five types of conferences in our writing workshop: a Drafting Conference, Revising/Editing Conference, Goal-Setting Conference, and a Sharing Conference.

DRAFTING CONFERENCE

Many students are eager to share their writing at various stages of completion. Drafting conferences offer students the chance to talk over these works-in-progress with a teacher. A quick check-in at the beginning of writing workshop shows us where writers are in their pieces and lets us see who might need our help in getting started with a new piece of writing. To keep things focused, one of the first questions we ask the writer is, "What do you need?" or "How is your writing going?" Then, based on the student feedback, we determine a focus for the conference. It may be part of a piece, or it may be a conversation that inspires the student to continue working on a piece of writing. Don't underestimate the power of a drafting conference to get things started. Simply asking, "What have you been writing about lately?" or "What would you be interested in writing more about today?" is a good way to get a writer's creative juices flowing.

One of the strengths of these conferences is that they can be initiated by writers, when they see the need, or by you if you feel that a little boost might help keep a writer going. Building collaboration during the drafting phase of the process reminds your students that they aren't alone even at the first-draft stage.

Keys to an Effective Drafting Conference

❋ Establish a purpose by asking questions such as:

- How's it going?
- What do you need to keep you going?
- Do you need an idea to get started with your writing?
- Do you need to talk about what you've written so far to keep you going?
- Are you stuck? Do you need to talk to someone to get you "unstuck"?

❋ Ask the writer to articulate the next step he or she will take in the writing process.

❋ Write down on a sticky note any ideas related to next steps the student might take.

❋ Make any notes that may help you with future planning with the student or planning a mini-lesson for the whole class.

REVISING CONFERENCE

Many students have told us that they don't need a conference for revision because their writing is "just fine!" Then, believe it or not, when they sit with us at our conferring table, they realize that their piece does need some work after all!

Revising conferences come when a writer has a completed piece that is ready to be shared with others. Writers may make some revisions on their own, but they often need help to complete the job. We enjoy the opportunity to discuss revision with our students. We want them to understand that

Keys to an Effective Revising Conference

❊ Set a purpose—focus on revising a specific aspect of the written piece.

❊ When revising, some questions might be the following:

- How's it going? What would you like to do to make your piece better?

- Let's read your piece aloud. How does it sound? Are there any words that you'd like to change to make it better?

- As you look at your piece, would you like to make any changes to how it is organized to make it easier for your reader to understand?

- As you look and listen to your sentences, do they read fluently? Do they start differently? Can you make the sentences in your piece flow better?

❊ Choose a portion of the piece to revise together. Then assign a portion of the piece for the student to revise independently. At your next meeting, review that work together and then, if needed, practice revising another portion together again.

❊ Make notes after each revision conference to inform future lesson planning for whole-group revision lessons. This can allow you to see patterns in your students as they grow and develop throughout the year.

revision is an important part of the writing process. Taking time in the conference setting to talk about writing and how to improve it through revision is a valuable use of our teaching time.

Sometimes, when writers are overwhelmed by both revision and editing within the same piece of writing, it is more manageable to focus the conference on a particular skill or strategy: "Would you like to focus on word choice or sentence fluency?" The teacher and the learner can then start the revision process together, with the writer responsible for completing the changes independently.

EDITING CONFERENCE

After students have made revisions to their writing piece, they are ready to make final editing changes. This is the last stage of the writing process, and it is where writers do the work of editors, fine-tuning the writing for their readers.

At an editing conference, a teacher can sit with the student and ask him or her to edit a particular piece of writing using an editor's checklist with grammar and mechanics skills that have been taught in mini-lessons (See editing checklist, p. 67). For your reluctant writers who might become overwhelmed by all the items on an editor's checklist, ask, "What items on the list would you like to edit this piece for today?" Creating a manageable checklist is a great way to ensure student success.

Remember, the goal of an editing conference is to help students edit their writing so it is comprehensible to the reader. Preparing for the final draft or publishing phase of the writing process helps writers understand the audiences for whom they are writing and create pieces that are understandable.

Keys to an Effective Editing Conference

❋ Set a purpose—focus on editing the written piece.

❋ When editing, some questions might be the following:

- How's it going? What would you like to do to make your piece better?

- Let's read your piece aloud. How does it sound? Does it sound the way you want it to sound?

- Are all of your sentences complete thoughts?

- How does the punctuation make the writing sound? Does your piece need some more punctuation marks at the end of your sentences? Does it need some different punctuation marks at the end of your sentences?

- Do some of your sentences need any other punctuation marks? What kinds? Commas? Quotation marks? Ellipses?

- Do you have capital letters in the words that need them?

- Does your spelling interfere with the reader's ability to understand your writing?

❋ Choose a portion of the piece to edit together. Then assign a portion of the piece for the student to edit independently. At your next meeting, review the work together and then, if needed, practice editing another portion together again.

❋ Make notes after each editing conference to inform future lesson planning for whole-group editing lessons. This can allow you to see patterns in your students as they grow and develop throughout the year.

GOAL-SETTING CONFERENCE

During goal-setting conferences, in which teachers and students meet to discuss writing goals, students list their various writing projects and each project's stages of completion on a Writing Record Sheet (see online resources, p. 160). At scheduled times, like the end of grading periods, the teacher and the student look at these projects together. As they review the writing, students fill out the Goal-Setting Form for Writing and formulate a goal based on their observations. As students gain familiarity with this process, they may fill out the form in advance to allow more time for discussion.

We enjoy doing goal setting with our students because it gives us an opportunity to take a holistic look at a range of students' writing. We reinforce the language that we use in our mini-lessons as we discuss and choose skills or strategies the student would like to work on.

As we look at not only instruction within our own classrooms, but across the grade levels from kindergarten through high school, the standards set clear expectations for writers and give teachers specific language to use with students to help them set achievable goals.

Keys to an Effective Goal-Setting Conference

❋ Create a culture of goal setting within your writing workshop.

❋ Invite students to look at writing samples—either within their writer's notebook, their writing folder, or published writing pieces—and identify areas that they would like to work on.

Here are some examples of student writing goals:

- Improving writing in a specific writing form (narrative, expository, argument)

- Generating ideas in a writer's notebook to help with creating writing pieces

- Understanding the purpose of revision and how it improves written pieces

- Maintaining and using an editing checklist to make sure readers can read and understand each piece

❋ As students leave a goal-setting conference, give them a copy of their completed goal-setting form so that they can see it daily. Keep copies for yourself so that you can refer to them when you touch base with students in upcoming writing conferences to see how they are progressing toward meeting their writing goals.

My Goal Setting Plan

Name _____ Date _____

What I'm doing well . . . _____

What I'd like to do better . . . _____

My goal will be . . . _____

Someone who will help me meet my goal is . . . _____

They will help me meet my goal by . . . _____

I will know that I have met my goal when . . . _____

SHARING CONFERENCE

Sharing conferences provide opportunities for students to show writing to a teacher that they may not choose to publish. Sometimes this conversation helps writers decide if they are going to move forward with a piece and publish it. Or it may allow students to share a piece that they do not want to show their peers.

One benefit of sharing conferences is that they build a writer's confidence and foster a sense of agency. They also provide a time for you to give positive and descriptive feedback or offer an encouraging word when a student might not be expecting it. Newfound confidence can often send a writer on the way to finishing and publishing a piece that he or she wasn't originally planning on completing. It can also motivate readers to start something new.

Our favorite benefit of the sharing conference is building relationships with our student writers. As we look to create a writing community in our classrooms, we know that this starts with the connection between our writers and us. Sitting side by side with them and listening as they share their writing is one of the most important first steps to reaching the goal of a thriving reading community.

Sharing and Celebrating

> **Sharing and Celebrating** → *Sharing and celebrating are focused on reflection about how writers went about crafting their pieces, the process or strategies that were independently applied.*

Our students generally fall into two groups—those who can't wait to get up and share what they have written with their peers, and those who have an anxiety attack when it is their turn. Which group do you fall into? How can we create a safe environment where students are willing to take risks as writers? We want our classroom to be a place where students want to share their writing with us, with a partner, and even occasionally with the whole class. One way to check the barometer of your classroom writing community is to have an honest conversation with your students about the physical environment where they work on writing. Record their answers, then create classroom norms for sharing time for your writers.

- When do you like sharing your writing?

- How do you like sharing your writing? With a partner? With a small group? With the whole class?

- How do you feel when you share your writing?

- What kind of feedback helps you as a writer? How do you like to receive feedback about your writing? Orally or written?

- What kinds of comments are helpful in improving your writing? What kinds of questions are helpful in improving your writing? (See box at right for some helpful comments and questions for writers.)

Questions/Feedback for Student Writers

- ❋ What did you notice about the writing?

- ❋ Tell the writer something he or she did well in the piece.

- ❋ Name a strategy that the writer used in his or her writing.

- ❋ What was something new that you did in your piece that you haven't done before?

- ❋ Name something that this writer did that you have also done as a writer.

- ❋ Name something that this writer did that you'd like to try.

- ❋ What is a favorite word or phrase in the piece?

Once you've created class norms, record them on a chart so that students can refer to them during writing workshop time. Regularly ask students if they want to add or change the norms as they have had opportunities to share with one another and with the class. We find that if students feel that they have a say in the creation and maintenance of the norms, they are more invested in maintaining them.

Looking Back, Moving Forward

Writing Workshop is one of our favorite times, of the school day and of the school year. It reminds us what is really important about writing and writing instruction. In a day and age when test prep and test writing overwhelms both teachers and students, the most important thing we can give our writers is time to write, time to talk about their writing, and time to celebrate their writing every day!

As you transition to Part 2, you will continue to transform your teaching by adding the essential routines offered in Chapter 5 and inquiry experiences explored in Chapters 6 and 7 to the new essentials for literacy teaching that you learned about in the first section. Each teaching routine and inquiry experience addresses a key teaching goal along with specific learning targets. As you guide students through these routines and experiences, revisit the overarching, cross-curricular targets (see box) that we want our students to master in order to become independent, self-directed learners.

> ❋ I can PAUSE
>
> ❋ I can PONDER
>
> ❋ I can look for PATTERNS
>
> ❋ I can PROBLEM SOLVE
>
> ❋ I can be PRECISE
>
> ❋ I can communicate my PROCESS
>
> ❋ I can PERSEVERE
>
> *(Walther, 2015)*

When you weave these learning experiences into your reading and writing workshops, you help your students reach higher standards while also encouraging them to be thoughtful readers and writers whose skills reflect essential literacy practices. The goal is for students to do the following:

- Make sense of complex text and persevere in figuring it out.
- Reason abstractly and *qualitatively.*
- Construct logical, evidence-based arguments and critique the reasoning of others.
- Think by writing.
- Use structures of text, text features, and digital resources strategically.
- Comprehend and communicate with precision.
- Look for and make use of structure express regularity in repeated reasoning.

To assist you as you plan, the descriptions of both the teaching routines and the inquiry experiences follows the same format. For many of the routines and experiences, you will find a suggested text or two that will lead your students to the learning in the standards. Keep in mind these texts are not the only resources you can use. We are sure you have a collection of books and online resources that work well for teaching certain lessons or concepts. As you read through the experiences in this part of the book, think about where those tried-and-true texts will enhance the experience. More important, when making key instructional choices regarding resources to support your students' learning, consider both their interests and individual needs.

The Components of Teaching Routines and Inquiry Experiences

TARGETS

Learning targets, written in kid-friendly language, will lead students toward key understandings stipulated in the standards. Targets set the stage and help students understand the significance of the learning.

PREPARATION

The success of the experience depends on preparation. Start with carefully selected books that can serve as exemplar texts and, later, add selections of your own.

EXPLANATION

Identifying the rationale for the experience is valuable during conversations with colleagues, administrators, students and their families, or when you are documenting your decision-making process for a teacher evaluation.

EXPERIENCE

The big ideas that children gain from these inquiry experiences resemble separate threads that, when woven together, create a rich tapestry of instruction.

Chapter 5

Teaching Routines

The teaching routines that follow are designed to be engaging, purposeful, and ongoing. They will help you do the following:

- Establish a literacy community

- Integrate foundational and language skills

- Spotlight vivid vocabulary

Go online to view a video on Teaching Routines in Action. See page 160 for details.

With a clear purpose and your end goals in mind, you will teach skills and strategies within each reading and writing experience. It is up to you to be responsive to the needs and interests of your students, continually adjusting the routines based on your formative assessments and observations. As you fine-tune these instructional practices with your learners in mind, each experience will become even more relevant and meaningful.

Big Idea: Establish a Literacy Community

Creating and maintaining a literacy community in our classrooms begins on the first day of school and continues until the last. Within this community, we want our students not only to reach the learning targets set in the standards, but also to be motivated to become lifelong readers and writers. With practice, these routines will become part of your teaching repertoire, and you will begin to incorporate these learning targets, and many more, on your own.

Share Book Recommendations

Book-talking time is one of the key components of building a reading community with our students. When we plan for our book talks, we make a point of sharing a wide range of text types so that students have lots of choices to add to their Someday Lists.

A Few of Our Favorite Books for Beginning-of-the-Year Book Talks

Title, Author	Brief Summary
Wonder (Palacio, 2013)	Homeschooled because of a severe facial deformity, Auggie Pullman suddenly finds himself in a mainstream fifth-grade classroom. Told in multiple voices, this story dramatizes Auggie's challenges as well as those faced by people in Auggie's world during one very special year.
Ungifted (Korman, 2012)	Donovan Curtis plays the biggest prank of his middle school career and somehow ends up in the gifted school. As he struggles to maintain his academic "secret," he finds himself drawn to the students preparing for a robotics contest.
The Year of Billy Miller (Henkes, 2013)	Billy ends his summer vacation with an accident that could affect his memory, but he is determined to have an amazing year. He wants to be a better student, get along with his sister, and be a bigger help at home.
Because of Mr. Terupt (Buyea, 2010)	Mr. Terupt, a new teacher, has high hopes for his first class. Learning how to get along and then experiencing tragedy brings his students together in a way that they never expected.

TARGET

I can select books based on recommendations from my teacher and other trusted readers.

PREPARATION

Gather a variety of high-interest books to use for weekly book talks. Discussing even just a book or two each week helps readers add titles to their Someday Lists and gives them choices to select from during their independent reading time.

EXPLANATION

At the beginning of the year we talk about the habits of experienced readers. One such habit is making reading plans. Thus, book talks serve a valuable function for our readers, introducing them to a variety of books from which to choose. These talks also allow us to familiarize students with books related to curriculum topics that will help move them up the ladder of text complexity as the year progresses.

EXPERIENCE

Our book talks may center on a particular genre, such as realistic fiction or fantasy, or a curricular topic like astronomy, the Civil War, or Abraham Lincoln. Sometimes we simply discuss new titles that we think will be of interest to our readers. Our goal is to hook them without giving away too much about the plot, especially the ending, so they will want to pick the book up and read it or put it on their Someday List. A sample book talk for one of our favorite books, *A Snicker of Magic* by Natalie Lloyd (2014), is below. Eventually, as our readers develop their own reading preferences and get to know one another as readers, they begin to have book talks of their own, sharing favorite titles and recommending titles to each other. Donalyn Miller and Susan Kelley (2013) say this is how our reading communities should develop with intermediate readers. The goal is for them to begin to depend on one another for book recommendations and not the teacher. After all, we will not always be there to recommend a title—but hopefully a trusted friend will.

Sample Book Talk Based on *A Snicker of Magic*

Today I'm going to share a book with you. It's one that I enjoyed and I think that some of you might enjoy reading, too. *A Snicker of Magic* by Natalie Lloyd is a fantasy book with some characters that many of you can probably relate to. Felicity is a 12-year-old girl who moves to Midnight Gulch with her family. Her family moves often, and she hopes that this will be the place that they'll stay. Felicity has a unique gift: she is a "word collector." She sees words wherever she goes, words about all the people she meets, and she "collects" those words. Wouldn't that be a neat gift to have? Midnight Gulch is a magical place, but its magic is about to run out. Felicity and her new friend, Jonah, may be the only ones who can solve the mystery that is draining the magic from Midnight Gulch. But her family might be moving again before she can help solve the mystery. Will she be able to stay in a place that she has begun to love, and will she be able to keep the magic in Midnight Gulch? If you'd like to find out, you really should read this book. It's one of my favorites, and I think it could be one of yours, too.

Develop Reading Preferences

TARGETS

- I can identify what text type(s) I like to read.
- I can choose text types beyond my preferences.

PREPARATION

- Create an interest survey or use a published one like the one found in *Next Step Guided Reading Assessment* (Richardson & Walther, 2013).

- Create an ongoing anchor chart to record and discuss the genres that you introduce through book talks or read-alouds or that students share from their independent reading.

- Assemble genre-based text sets and have book talks based on them to encourage students to

Reading Genres

FICTION

Realistic Fiction: A made-up story with characters or events that could actually happen in real life.

Historical Fiction: A fictional story set during a historical time period.

Fantasy: A story where characters and events have magical or fantasy-like characteristics, such as talking animals.

Science Fiction: A story that uses science or technology as part of the setting or plot of the story and is often set in the future.

Mystery: A story where characters use clues to help solve a central problem by the end.

Traditional Literature: Stories passed down through the oral tradition of storytelling, such as myths, fables, fairy tales, and folktales.

Graphic Novels: Like comic books, they tell a story in sequence using illustrations, characters, and speech bubbles to communicate what happens.

NONFICTION

Informational Text: Words written to describe or explain an aspect of the natural or social world, primarily told through text and photographs.

Biography: The story of a real person's life.

Autobiography: The story of a real person's life, written by that person.

POETRY

Poetry: Text written in verse that may or may not rhyme.

DRAMA

Play: A story told through scripted dialogue between characters, intended for performance in a theater rather than just for reading.

read in unfamiliar genres; they can add the titles to their Someday Lists. For sample multi-genre sets, see page 41.

EXPLANATION

By building students' confidence, giving them a range of choices of text to read, and helping them create a reading plan, we prepare them to be lifelong readers. For some students, choosing books for their Someday List is an easy and natural process. Others need more explicit instruction. Miller and Kelley (2013) stress the importance of students developing reading preferences. If we do not help students do this, they may not be able to sustain their independent reading beyond the walls of our classrooms.

For students to develop reading preferences, they need exposure to a wide range of reading materials. Sometimes we gravitate to our favorite genres, authors, and titles, and this is a good place to start, especially if you are new to conducting book talks. But don't get too comfortable with your personal favorites. We are constantly reminding ourselves that not every reader in our classrooms is just like us! How do you ensure you're considering your readers' real preferences? Here are some useful strategies.

EXPERIENCE

Give students an interest survey to get a sense of not only what reading they enjoy but what their interests are. Continue to administer interest surveys every few months, because children's interests tend to change all the time. We often lack the time to gauge our students' latest fascinations, but these surveys can provide the hidden key that will us help match a student with a special book.

Our favorite saying is, "Know your reader, know your book." By doing both, you'll be able to satisfy even your pickiest readers. Assess your classroom library selections. Ask yourself, "Do I have a wide range of books for my students to choose from? Am I doing regular book-talks on a variety of genres with my students or am I stuck in a rut? Do my books reflect my students' preferences based on their survey results?" Do you need to refresh what is on your shelves by bringing in some new titles from the public library, or add other resources to replenish students' options? Keeping a watchful eye on the texts that are available to your students will help keep them engaged with their reading.

As you read aloud a book, discuss a text, or ask students about their current reading, add these titles to the ongoing genre chart that you are compiling. (Be aware that some books do not easily fit into a genre—what a great conversation that might be!)

During Status of the Class time, have students identify the genre or text type of their independent reading book, rate it on a scale of 1–10, and briefly explain the reasoning behind the rating.

Create Anchor Charts

TARGET

I can access information from mini-lessons whenever I need it.

PREPARATION

Gather materials to record student thinking. We prefer large sheets of white drawing paper (available from school supply catalogs) and sticky notes for students to use when writing their individual thinking for the anchor chart.

EXPLANATION

We begin the school year with empty classroom walls in anticipation of the anchor charts that we will build with our students. These charts will line the walls and provide students with valuable references throughout the year. Our anchor charts often begin with a question, such as "What is theme?" or "How do characters change over time?" Or we start with a big idea, such as comparing and contrasting two pieces of text. We like to use sticky notes because it allows all of our students to participate by adding to the chart and having their thinking displayed for all to see.

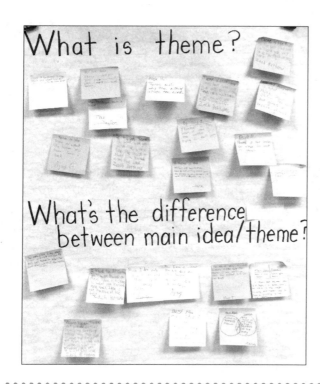

What is theme?

What's the difference between main idea/theme?

Alli

I find that many books that we've been reading have a theme that relates to believing and giving to one and other.

Create class anchor charts by having students record their thinking on sticky notes and attaching those notes to the chart.

EXPERIENCE

- Determine a purpose for the chart.
- As you discuss the topic, make notes and have students write their thinking on sticky notes. Add the notes to the anchor chart so that all thinking is represented on the chart. Remind students to include their name.
- Display the chart in the room for as long as it is useful to your students.
- Take a photo of the chart or type up the learning it contains so it can be reproduced and added to reading or writing notebooks.

Big Idea: Integrate Foundational and Language Skills

Even as intermediate teachers, we are responsible for teaching both foundational and language skills. Look for opportunities to integrate these skills throughout the day to make teaching them more manageable for you and learning them more cohesive for your students.

Develop Fluency

TARGET

I can read fluently and accurately to better understand my reading of both prose and poetry.

PREPARATION

- Choose short, engaging texts that motivate your readers to keep reading.

- Incorporate fluency practice into reading workshop as either a unit of study or as a five-to-ten-minute activity each week.

- Gather a variety of shorter texts for students to choose from for fluency practice.

EXPLANATION

Fluent readers have the ability to read accurately, at a reasonable rate, and with expression. Fluency relates to a student's success in comprehension and overall reading proficiency, both in oral and silent reading (Rasinski, 2012). Therefore, it is well worth our instructional time to teach students how to read fluently (not just "fast," a characteristic that some students inaccurately ascribe to fluent reading). An inaccurate perception among teachers is that fluency instruction is just for the primary grades. Even teachers of middle and high school students need to work with their students on fluency, especially with their students who struggle.

EXPERIENCE

Repeated readings are the key to developing fluency. These should be presented in a meaningful context wherein students can practice their skills and ultimately perform or share in authentic contexts. Here are some ways to foster fluency among your students:

- Host an open house for parents or guests where students share a special poem or other prepared reading that they have selected and rehearsed.

- Invite family, friends, or other classrooms to hear a readers' theater script read aloud. Readers' theater scripts are purely verbal and do not need props.

- Become "buddies" with a class of younger students. Once a month, your students can share a favorite poem with a buddy and then listen to the buddies read so they can improve their own fluency. The younger readers may bring poetry, a book, or piece of their own writing to read aloud to a partner. Remember the goal here is to build the relationship between your readers as well as to develop fluency.

- Get your classroom in the mood for poetry by assigning each student a poem, or part of a poem, to recite on a certain day as part of morning announcements. Record short stories or other picture books using a multimedia device and then add a musical soundtrack. These recordings make great gifts at holiday time or keepsakes for students!

Teach Word-Solving Strategies

TARGETS

- I can identify affixes (prefixes and suffixes).
- I can identify root words.
- I can understand how prefixes and suffixes change the meanings of root words.

PREPARATION

- Select a read-aloud that highlights affixes. A few of our favorites are on page 83.
- Make each child a prefix/suffix sheet (see page 83 and online resources, page 160).

 Transforming Literacy Teaching in the Era of Higher Standards, Grades 3–5 © 2015 by Karen Biggs-Tucker and Brian Tucker, Scholastic Teaching Resources

A Few of Our Favorite Books Teaching Prefixes/Suffixes

Title, Author	Brief Summary
Pre- and Re-, Mis- and Dis-: What Is a Prefix? (Cleary, 2013)	In simple terms, this book explains how prefixes work to change the meanings of root words.
-ful and –less, -er and –ness: What Is a Suffix? (Cleary, 2014)	Engaging illustrations and text explain how suffixes change the meanings of root words.
Cryptomania! Teleporting Into Greek and Latin With Cryptokids (Fine, 2004)	Join the Cryptokids on a fantasy trip and learn how Greek and Latin word origins exist in daily life.
Happy Endings: A Story About Suffixes (Pulver, 2011)	Confusion erupts when Mr. Wright announces his intention to tackle suffixes after lunch. Will the suffixes be able to convince the students that they are helpful?

EXPLANATION

In *Word Nerds: Teaching All Students to Learn and Love Vocabulary* (2013), Brenda Overturf and her colleagues stress the importance of teaching students morphemic awareness to help them make sense of multisyllabic words that they encounter in the core academic areas. Breaking apart words into root words and affixes is an effective way to help students develop this ability. When students have a working knowledge of Greek and Latin roots, their word knowledge and vocabularies grow because they have a better understanding of how words are related. As students begin to understand how prefixes and suffixes affect the meaning of words, it improves their ability to comprehend increasingly complex text in a variety of settings.

EXPERIENCE

- Read aloud the selected book to students.
- Complete the prefix/suffix chart, recording together several words from the book and discussing the nature of prefixes, root words, and suffixes.
- Determine the meaning of each identified word based on the information on the chart.
- Discuss how breaking down a word and looking at its parts helps readers unlock its meaning.
- Encourage students to add 3–5 words from their independent reading to the chart and share them with the whole class or in a reading conference.
- Repeat this experience multiple times throughout the year with increasingly complex texts, helping learners to see the prevalence of affixes and root words in the books they read and how word strategies can help them make meaning from those words.

Big Idea: Spotlight Vivid Vocabulary

Teaching vocabulary in context helps to engage learners in word learning. These routines actively involve students in discussing words, discovering connections between words, and incorporating new vocabulary into their day-to-day learning. As a result, students improve their ability to infer word meanings and comprehend complex texts.

Build Connections Between Words

TARGETS

- I can understand how words are related to one another.
- I can show my knowledge of word relationships in my reading, writing, listening, and speaking.

PREPARATION

Choose 6–8 words from a picture book, a novel, or a short piece of text that you are reading with the whole class and write them on a piece of chart paper. Share them with the group prior to reading the text aloud.

Tantalizing Titles With Rich Vocabulary

Title, Author	Brief Summary
City Cat (Banks, 2013)	A stray cat goes on the adventure of a lifetime as she joins a family on vacation in Europe and sees many of the sights of the continent.
Donavan's Word Jar (DeGross, 1994)	Donavan loves words and collects them in his word jar. As it fills up, he worries what he will do when there is no more room left. Will he lose all the words he's collected? It's a dilemma that no word lover ever wants to face.
The Boy Who Loved Words (Schotter, 2006)	Selig collects words—words that make him laugh and words that make him happy. But what will he do with them all? Give them away to others who need them, of course!
The Very Inappropriate Word (Tobin, 2013)	Michael is always on the lookout for interesting words. One day he finds a new one . . . but it is the wrong kind. When Michael decides to try it out at school, he discovers just how inappropriate a word can be!

EXPLANATION

In *Bringing Words to Life: Robust Vocabulary Instruction* (2013), Isabel Beck and her colleagues discuss the need for repeated exposures to words and word relationships in order for students to understand new vocabulary. As we think about the words that are being presented in the more complex texts students read in the content areas and in their day-to-day reading, it is imperative that we work on expanding their vocabularies. Helping students understand the relationships between words, both the new ones they are learning and the ones they already know, is essential for preparing them to be the readers and writers of the 21st century. Having a routine where students discover new words both in read-aloud experiences and in their own reading bolsters that vital word knowledge throughout the year.

EXPERIENCE

Beck and her colleagues suggest the following experience for highlighting the relationships between words:

- Share pairs of words prior to reading the text aloud. Encourage students to pay special attention to these words during the read-aloud.

- Afterward, present the words in pairs and ask students if the words connect to each other, and how. (There is no right answer here. Students just need to be able to support their thinking.)

- Continue with each pair of words. Discuss how each of the words may or may not have a connection to each other.

- Encourage students to look for pairs of words in their independent reading. Then have them share with a partner, then with the whole class, to discuss relationships between words.

Celebrate the Language of Poetry

TARGETS

- I can identify and interpret figurative words and phrases in a poem.
- I can explain how a poem is structured.
- I can explain how a speaker in a poem reflects on a topic.

PREPARATION

- Collect a variety of poems related to student interests, curricular topics, seasons, holidays, and so on.

- Reproduce the poems for students. Students can collect their poems in a binder or folder.

- Identify resources (both textual and digital) where students can begin to access and collect their own poems to share with partners, small groups, or the whole class as they begin to identify favorite poets and poetry forms, such as free verse, rhyming, and haiku.

EXPLANATION

Poetry collections provide students with a great way to practice fluency as well as develop vocabulary in a playful way. In *Teaching Struggling Readers With Poetry* (2010), Carol Fuhler and Maria Walther identify three important reasons to incorporate poetry into our reading workshop:

- Poetry plays with language.
- Poems consist of well-chosen words.
- Poetry contains rich vocabulary.

A Few of Our Favorite Poetry Books

Title, Author	Brief Summary
Touch the Poem (Adoff, 2000)	Poems focusing on the seasons of the year through the five senses—seeing, feeling, tasting, touching, and hearing.
The Goof Who Invented Homework and Other School Poems (Dakos, 1996)	A collection of humorous poems about events and emotions related to the school year.
I've Lost My Hippopotamus (Prelutsky, 2012)	Poems and illustrations about animals and other subjects presented in humorous and poetic styles to engage readers of all ages.
Today at the Bluebird Café (Ruddell, 2007)	A collection of poems focusing on characteristics of birds told in lyrical verse.
Rutherford B. Who Was He? Poems About Our Presidents (Singer, 2013)	Forty-three men with two things in common: Each was president of the United States and each inspired poetry in his honor. This engaging text is paired with interesting facts about the presidents.
Popcorn (Stevenson, 1998)	A collection of poems that are funny, thoughtful, and sometimes quirky about a variety of topics.

Provide opportunities for learners to practice fluency by reading poetry with partners.

EXPERIENCE

In a lesson on poetry, we focus on only one small aspect of poetry at a time. This way we can spend the majority of our time reading and discussing the poem, and encouraging an appreciation for poetry, which is the ultimate goal of our instruction.

- Identify your instructional focus for the poem.

- Pass out the selected poem to students.

- Have the whole class read the poem aloud with appropriate phrasing and expression.

- Encourage the students to read along with you in a subsequent reading (or readings) so they can get a feel for appropriate oral reading.

- Revisit the poem to notice and name key words, phrases, or figurative language (like those found in the box on page 87).

- Show students how to mark and label these words or phrases in the poem so they can refer to them later.

- Encourage students to reread the poem on their own, with a partner, or with someone at home to provide continued fluency practice and discuss what they've learned about the use of language in the poem.

Notice and Name Poetic Elements

Here are some poetic elements that you and your students will encounter as you explore poetry:

- ❋ *Rhythm*—use rhythm to emphasize words, suggest movement, or create mood
- ❋ *Rhyme*—gives poems their musical quality
- ❋ *Repetition*—repeated words or phrases emphasize meaning and/or create rhythm
- ❋ *Alliteration*—repetition of the beginning consonant
- ❋ *Onomatopoeia*—words that sound like the action or thing they represent
- ❋ *Sensory images*—appeal to the five senses and help readers make mental pictures
- ❋ *Simile*—comparison between two objects using "like" or "as"
- ❋ *Metaphor*—comparison between two objects or ideas, without using "like" or "as"
- ❋ *Meter*—the rhythm of a poem
- ❋ *Personification*—ascribing human characteristics to an animal or inanimate object
- ❋ *Creative use of conventions*—the use of dashes, italics, and various fonts for emphasis or effect within a poem

Fuhler & Walther (2010)

Looking Back, Moving Forward

These teaching routines establish and maintain the literacy community in our classrooms. Once we have established these routines so they can be repeated throughout the year—with increasingly complex text and increased expectations for students' skills in using them—we are ready to do the work of planning our inquiry experiences.

Chapter 6

Inquiry Experiences— Reading in Focus

The inquiry experiences in this chapter will integrate the language arts standards in a meaningful way in your reading and writing workshop. The big ideas in these experiences will focus your instruction on building independence for your readers as they develop their skills in reading, writing, listening, and speaking. Each experience can be repeated across the year with increasingly complex text and less scaffolding as students become more independent.

Go online to view a video on Inquiry Experiences— Reading in Action. See page 160 for details.

Think about the stages of inquiry and the stages of the gradual release model, which we synthesize on page 89. It is important to note that the stages, like the inquiry experiences themselves, are not linear. Students may need to move back and forth to deepen their understanding of a particular concept. Samantha Bennett (2007) and Debbie Miller (2013) describe this as the "catch and release" model rather than the gradual release model. We like this term because it captures the ebb and flow that exists in our workshop settings, where we teach, observe, reteach, observe, and repeat the cycle based on the needs of our students.

As you begin to implement these inquiry experiences in your classroom, take time to observe and

Stages of Inquiry (Harvey & Daniels, 2009)	Stages of Gradual Release (Pearson & Gallagher, 1983)
IMMERSE • Invite curiosity • Build background • Find topics • Wonder	**TEACHER MODELING AND DEMONSTRATION** • Read-aloud • Think-aloud • Demonstration writing • Scaffolded conversations
INVESTIGATE • Develop questions • Search for information • Discover answers	**GUIDED PRACTICE** • Shared/interactive reading and writing • Guided reading and writing • Partner reading and writing • Individual reading and writing conferences
COALESCE • Intensify research • Synthesize information • Build knowledge	**INDEPENDENT PRACTICE** • Independent reading, writing, and conferring
GO PUBLIC • Share learning • Demonstrate understanding • Take action	**APPLICATION IN AUTHENTIC CONTEXTS** • Share learning • Demonstrate understanding • Take action

A Common Sense View of Gradual Release

Ongoing Assessment and Celebration

TEACHER MODELING AND DEMONSTRATION
"I Show You"

SHARED DEMONSTRATION
"We Do It"

GUIDED PRACTICE WITH DESCRIPTIVE FEEDBACK
"You Try It"

INDEPENDENT APPLICATION
"You Apply It"

Adapted from: Pearson & Gallagher, 1983; Miller, 2013; Routman, 2008

listen to your students; they will teach you everything you need to know as you strive to make the learning relevant and meaningful.

Big Idea: Read (and Read Some More!)

We are believers in backward planning, so we begin with the end in mind. Our ultimate goal is to have students apply their accumulated knowledge from all their learning experiences to any text they read. In this section, we'll share two inquiry experiences designed to help students make sense of increasingly complex text.

The standards require that readers be operating at a high level and keep improving. In fact, "The Reading Standards place equal emphasis on the sophistication of what students read and the skill with which they read" (NGA Center and CCSSO, 2010, p. 31). The CCSS is the first standards document that addresses students' ability to read increasingly complex text over the grades (Hiebert & Pearson, 2013). It requires that the grade-level texts (as designated by the CCSS) that students read at the end of the year be more challenging than those read at the beginning. This requirement has probably caused more anxiety for teachers than any other part of the standards. How do we accomplish this goal?

The answer is simple and complex at the same time—read! Giving students time each day to read is one of the most powerful tools that we have to help steadily increase their capacity to read complex texts. Students who read during the day build their reading stamina and motivation to read more, not only at school but at home, too!

Inquiry Experience: Build a Ladder of Text Complexity

TARGET

I can read and comprehend a variety of complex texts.

PREPARATION

Students will need their "Books I've Read" list and a Reading Ladder form (see page 91 and online resources, page 160).

EXPLANATION

Text complexity has become a buzzword as a direct result of the Common Core State Standards. We have introduced the term to our students, explaining that it has two meanings. The first, the "CCSS meaning," relates to our goal that all students be able to read grade-level texts by the end of the year. The second meaning is different for each student and reflects the fact that each reader will progress toward more complex text based on his or her current level.

EXPERIENCE

Modeling and Demonstration

Starting on the first day of school, we discuss how students challenge themselves as readers in both whole-class conversations and individual goal-setting conferences. Familiarizing students with different titles at various levels of complexity is one way to help them better grasp the concept; see the chart below for a list of qualities we introduce to students. Using three or four books in the same genre, we show students how they can move from an easier book to one that's more complex. (See some text sets leveled by complexity and student interest on page 42.)

Guided Practice

Next, students practice ordering texts by complexity on their own. This can be done one-on-one in a conference or in a small-group setting. Have students bring three or four titles that they have read and order them by level of text complexity. Then have them talk among themselves or with you as to why they have ordered the books as they have. These conversations will give you insight into your students as readers, as well as help students think about the kinds of books they can read on their way up the text complexity ladder.

Self-Assessing Text Complexity as a Reader

QUALITATIVE	• Do I understand this text?
	• Can I navigate the structure of this text?
QUANTITATIVE	• Can I read most of the words in the text?
	• Do I understand most of the words (vocabulary) in this text?
MATCHING READER TO TASK	• Is this a text that I want to read?
	• Is this appropriate for me as a reader?
	• Do I have the life experiences/schema to understand/appreciate this text?

Independent Practice and Application

To complete a "Reading Ladder of Text Complexity," students will do the following:

1. Select several books from their Books I've Read list (5–7 titles is ideal, but any number can work).

2. Order the titles from the least complex to most complex, explaining what about the title made it challenging or helped students grow as readers.

3. With a partner or in a reading conference, discuss their understanding of text complexity and how it is reflected in their own personal reading.

Repeat this task every month, every grading period, or whenever best meets your needs and those of your students.

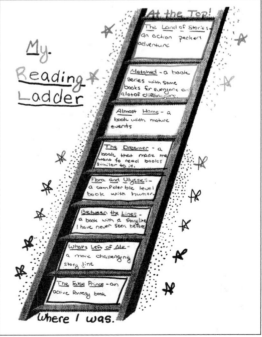

Teach readers to reflect and self-assess the complexity of their independent reading books.

Inquiry Experience: Read Self-Selected Books

TARGETS

- I can plan my independent reading time.
- I can choose books to read at school and at home.

PREPARATION

- Continue to build your classroom library. Refer to suggestions on pages 35–36 for creating a library for your readers. Remember that, along with your own books, you can stock your library with titles borrowed from the school and public libraries to match the interests of your readers.
- Determine a system for readers to record their independent reading. Create logs such as "Books I've Read" or "Someday List" (see page 50) as examples for collecting book titles during independent reading time at home and at school.
- Continue to present a wide variety of books through book talks to keep your students motivated to read texts in different genres of increasing complexity.

EXPLANATION

Too often, as students get older, some of them lose their love of reading. We believe we can keep the joy in our students by allowing them to choose what they read, sharing lots of great books, and teaching them to plan future reading with Someday Lists.

How to Keep Middle-Grade Readers Motivated to Read

- ❈ Get to know readers through interest and attitude surveys.
- ❈ Confer with students as often as possible.
- ❈ Match students to books that interest them.
- ❈ Share a wide variety of books through weekly book talks, exposing students to fiction, nonfiction, poetry, and even drama.
- ❈ Give students choice in books they read during independent reading time.
- ❈ Provide time daily for students to read their self-selected books independently.
- ❈ Encourage students to share what they are reading together. Book recommendations from peers are a great resource for Someday Lists.

EXPERIENCE

Modeling and Demonstration

Students come to us with a broad range of skills when it comes to choosing books for themselves. From the first day of school, we model how we go about choosing books and how we prioritize them on our Someday Lists. Taking the time to share our reading lives with our students is important

Professional Books That Have Helped Shape Our Planning of Independent Reading Time

❊ *No More Independent Reading Without Support* (Miller & Moss, 2013)

❊ *Quantity and Quality: Increasing the Volume and Complexity of Students' Reading* (Wilde, 2014)

❊ *Reading in the Wild: The Book Whisperer's Keys to Cultivating Lifelong Reading Habits* (Miller & Kelley, 2013)

❊ *The Reading Zone: How to Help Kids Become Skilled, Passionate, Habitual, Critical Readers* (Atwell, 2007)

Teach readers how to plan their daily independent reading.

as we begin to establish our reading community. When they see us modeling the importance of choosing books, reading books, and adding books to our Someday Lists, they see the value in that daily practice. You may want to create a chart like the one below that summarizes some of the ways readers choose books.

Guided Practice

Next, we work with individuals or small groups to explore the books in our classroom or building libraries and look for books that are just right for them. We often find it helpful to pull books out into baskets for small groups to look at in our classroom. This way, students can browse sections of our libraries more easily and may be able to find titles from a certain genre or author grouped together. We encourage students to add to their Someday Lists during these explorations and to share their lists with one another.

Independent Practice

- During reading workshop, students read self-selected books from the classroom library or titles recommended by teachers or students.

- After finishing a book, they write the title on their Books I've Read list. This list provides the teacher and the student with a reference to use in conferences, for goal setting, or for any other reading response.

- When students identify a book they would like to read later, they add it to their Someday List, a practice that encourages learners to rely on themselves, not on the teacher, when they finish a book.

Does a Book Belong on Your Someday List?

❊ Is it part of a series you love or one by a favorite author?

❊ Is it about a topic you are interested in?

❊ Was it recommended by a teacher or a reader who knows your reading preferences?

❊ Does it have an interesting cover and blurb?

❊ Does it have an intriguing book trailer or review?

❊ Did it capture your attention in another, unexpected way?

Matching Books to Readers

If students like . . .	Title, Author
Fantasy	*The Candymakers* (Mass, 2010)
Mystery	*The Homemade Stuffing Caper: Book 1* (Charlie Collier, Snoop for Hire) (Madormo, 2012)
Adventure	*Escape From Mr. Lemoncello's Library* (Grabenstein, 2013)
Realistic Fiction	*Absolutely Almost* (Graff, 2014)
Historical Fiction	*One Came Home* (Timberlake, 2013)
Science Fiction	*Star Wars: Jedi Academy* (Brown, 2013)

Big Idea: Engage in Collaborative Conversations

TRANSFORMING TEACHING	
Teachers mainly lead the questioning and discussion of texts.	Students mainly leading the questioning and discussion. Students are asking and answering questions about the text itself, as well as about the thinking of others to deepen their own understanding of the text.

Collaborative conversations are a critical part of the learning that occurs in reading and writing workshop as well as throughout the school day. Talk in the classroom is one of our most underutilized instructional tools. Our students are talking all the time; our challenge as teachers is to find a way to channel all their talk into productive forms of communication. The Common Core Standards for Listening and Speaking emphasize the importance of taking the time to "prepare students to participate effectively in a range of conversations and collaborations with diverse partners . . ." (NGA Center and CCSSO, 2010, p. 22). When we hurry through our instructional day trying to cover all the material that we need to teach, we often neglect to prepare students for the work required to achieve rich communication with one another. We need to invest the time and effort to teach them how to do this important work.

Inquiry Experience: Connect My Ideas

TARGETS

- I can ask and answer questions with a partner.
- I can build on the ideas of a partner.

PREPARATION

- Strategically group students in partnerships for initial "turn and talk" experiences. Consider pairing students who might need support with learners who are stronger in speaking/listening skills, as a means of providing valuable modeling. Once students have practiced the behaviors and expectations of talking with a partner, they can then choose their own partners or turn and talk with a neighbor while seated at desks or on the carpet during a read-aloud time.

- Make a chart with questions like the ones at right for students to refer to as they begin practicing. Students can also glue this list in their reader's notebook to consult during collaborative conversations. As students become more proficient, they will become less dependent on the chart and better able to participate naturally in partner and group discussions.

- Gather resources for students to read and discuss with their partners, such as the following:
  - ❋ Articles related to content-area topics
  - ❋ Different texts on the same topic (e.g., bullying, friendship, perseverance)
  - ❋ Multimedia sources, such as websites related to current topics
  - ❋ Independent reading books

- Create a text-dependent question or two for students to think about as they are reading. To prepare for the discussion, encourage them to take notes or to write on the text, if appropriate.

EXPLANATION

Collaborative conversations allow students to process their ideas and new information, listen to others as they do the same, and then revise their own thinking as they link their ideas to the thinking of their peers. Their understanding develops as they allow the ideas of others to permeate their own. As an added benefit, when students talk about their experiences with others, they strengthen their own thought

Encourage students to connect their ideas to the thinking of their classmates.

Connecting My Ideas to the Thinking of a Partner

- ❋ What do you think?
- ❋ Why do you think that?
- ❋ How do you know that?
- ❋ What questions do you still have?
- ❋ Can you tell more about your thinking?
- ❋ My ideas are similar to yours because . . . .
- ❋ My ideas are different from yours because . . . .
- ❋ I have questions about your thinking. They are . . . .

(Adapted from: Walther & Phillips, 2012)

processes by articulating ideas clearly so their partner can follow their thinking. It is important to remind students that there are not necessarily "right" answers in these types of conversations and that they need to be open to the ideas of others. Even intermediate students can struggle with taking turns and listening to others' ideas, so providing time for them to practice these skills is vital to the success of conversations.

EXPERIENCE

Modeling and Demonstration

- Introduce the Connect My Ideas strategy by explaining that the purpose of the strategy is for learners to share their thoughts together. Point out that hearing the thinking of others improves our own thought process by showing us new ways of thinking.

- Next, as you refer to the chart, reinforce how using these questions and statements encourages partners to explain their thinking and support it with reasons and text evidence. Point out how they ask students to compare and contrast their ideas with those of their partners—in a respectful, thoughtful way.

- Model with a student (or another adult, if possible) what it looks and sounds like when two people share their thinking and connect thoughts together. Have students identify the questions that you and your partner used during your conversation.

- Finally, reflect on how this process made your thinking better as you each shared your ideas and asked and answered questions together.

Guided Practice

- Before you read a text aloud to your students, state the purpose of the conversation that will follow. Remind students to look for evidence in the text to support and deepen their thinking, which is the ultimate goal of these collaborative conversations .

- Read aloud the selected text.

- Restate the purpose of the conversation and invite partners to begin their discussion, referring to the prompts as necessary.

- Circulate as students are discussing the text to see how their conversations are going and offer support as needed. Don't forget to respond to what they're doing with descriptive feedback to reinforce expectations of future turn-and-talk conversations. Here are more suggestions to foster positive partner talk:

    ❊ Encourage partners to listen to each other. Have them look for ways to connect their ideas as well as to ask and answer questions during their time together.

    ❊ Require students to support each point they make with evidence from the text. (Experienced speakers can explain their thinking by referring to the text or their notes.)

- After the discussion is complete, allow students a chance to process the activity. Ask the following questions:

    ❊ What went well in your conversation? What did you do well? What could you do better next time?

    ❊ Did your conversation help reinforce your ideas? Did you revise your thinking based on your conversation? How did connecting your ideas to others help you better understand the text you read?

- Work together with the class to create an anchor chart of strategies for turn-and-talk like the one on page 98.

A Collaborative Conversation Modeling
Connecting My Thinking to a Partner's

If you were going to demonstrate a collaborative conversation with your students during a read-aloud experience, it might look like something like this.

❋ Show the cover of the book *Telephone* (Barnett, 2014) or another text and ask, "What do you notice about the cover of the book? How does the illustration on the cover help you think about what the story might be about?"

❋ Invite a partner to help you model good "turn and talk" behaviors. (You may want to discuss strategies for building conversations with the student and/or practice the model conversation before the demonstration.) Show students how to connect their thinking to their partner's thinking by having a conversation like the following:

Teacher: What do you think the book is about?

Partner: I think that it's about some animals who might use a telephone to talk to each other.

Teacher: Why do you think that?

Partner: Because there are animals and a telephone pole on the cover. When I see that, I think about making a phone call to someone.

Teacher: I agree with your idea about making a phone call to someone. When I make a phone call to someone, it is usually because I have something important to tell that person. How about you? Do you think the characters have something important to tell each other?

Partner: I like your thinking. I called my grandparents when I won my soccer tournament. I wonder if the characters have good news that they want to share with someone. What do you think that their good news might be?

Teacher: I don't know, but I agree with you that making a phone call is a great way to communicate with someone about something important. I can't wait to read more in this book to see what these characters are communicating.

Partner: Me either! Thanks for sharing your thinking with me. It helped me make my thinking better by connecting my ideas to yours.

Teacher: Me too! Thanks for sharing your thinking with me, too! I can't wait to read more about what happens in this book. The cover sure looks interesting, and I bet the book is, too!

❋ Have students report to you what they have noticed you and your partner doing that demonstrated effective communication skills during your partner conversation.

Strategies for a Great Turn-and-Talk

❋ Face your partner during your conversation.

❋ Make eye contact with your partner.

❋ Listen to your partner.

❋ Be ready to talk when it is your turn.

❋ Talk only when it is your turn to talk.

❋ Speak so that only your partner can hear you.

❋ Respect the thoughts and ideas being shared by your partner.

❋ Turn and face the front when you and your partner are finished.

❋ Sit quietly when you are finished.

Independent Practice and Application

Have students connect their ideas throughout the year in reading, writing, math, content-area studies, or any time you want them to extend their thinking with a partner. Continue to provide opportunities for students to hone their conversational skills throughout the year. In addition, review the anchor chart frequently and add new questions that might be a good addition to conversations. These experiences help build students' independence so they are better able to participate in collaborative conversations with limited teacher involvement, as the next inquiry experience describes.

Inquiry Experience: Converse With Others

TARGETS

• I can prepare for a collaborative conversation by reading material to be discussed with a small group.

• I can listen to the thinking of others.

• I can ask and answer questions from others.

• I can build on the ideas of others.

PREPARATION

• Create a place where small groups can meet for discussions. Depending on the size of your classroom, this may be a small cluster of desks or an area on the carpet.

• Gather resources for students to read and discuss with their small groups, such as the following:

  ❋ Articles related to content-area topics

  ❋ Different texts on the same topic (e.g., bullying, friendship, perseverance)

  ❋ Multimedia sources, such as websites related to current topics

  ❋ Independent reading books

• Encourage students to find their own resources for a topic of their choice. This is a great way to release responsibility after they have had experiences where you provided texts for them. When they are reading, help them locate a text that group members can read prior to their collaborative conversations.

EXPLANATION

As students' collaborative conversations deepen, they will begin to challenge each other's thinking and defend their own. This is the next step in the discussion process. Intermediate learners also need to practice coming to their group having read the text and being prepared to discuss it.

EXPERIENCE

Modeling and Demonstration

- Demonstrate with two or three other adults what a collaborative conversation looks and sounds like. Students need to see that many of the same rules of partner sharing apply in a small-group collaborative conversation.

- Have students discuss what they observed:

  ❋ What did you notice about how the discussion looked and sounded in a small group?

  ❋ In what ways was it similar to having a conversation with a partner?

  ❋ How was it different?

- Invite students to notice that in many ways the conversations were the same. Making eye contact, active listening, and taking turns talking are important behaviors to reinforce as your students move from conversing with a partner to talking with two or three other students.

- Create an anchor chart with students of what collaborative conversation circles with three to five students would look and sound like. (See example at right.)

Guided Practice

- Have each group read the shared text.

- Strategically place students in small groups to practice conversation circles. (You might use the same considerations as you did when grouping students in partnerships.) Begin these conversations with a compelling read-aloud and a text-dependent question or two to get your students talking. Remember that the goal of collaborative conversations is for students to be "connecting their ideas" with someone else's thinking. As you listen to each group, guide their conversations if necessary by referring to the discussion prompts (see p. 95)—but try not to get involved too much. Remind students that the goal is for everyone to share their thinking at least once during the conversation so that every voice is heard. You may prompt them to do the following:

  ❋ Listen to others in the group, look for ways to connect their ideas, and look for questions to ask during their time together.

  ❋ Support each point that they make with evidence from the text.

  ❋ Ask and answer questions during the discussion to better understand other speakers taking part in the conversation.

- Reflect with students on what they did well and what they might do better next time.

Guidelines for a Successful Conversation-Circle Discussion

- ❋ Listen carefully and think carefully about the question to be discussed.

- ❋ Decide who will begin the conversation.

- ❋ Listen carefully to the person who is talking. Think about what is being said.

- ❋ Think about what you might want to add to others' thinking.

- ❋ If you want to add something or ask a question of the speaker, say the person's name first and then add your thinking or ask your question.

- ❋ Invite people into the conversation who have not shared by saying their name and asking what they think.

- ❋ Always respect the thinking of everyone in the group.

- ❋ When finished, thank the members of your group.

Independent Practice

After students have had practice in conversing both in partnerships and in small groups, look for chances for them to have more dialogue in their conversation circles. This helps prepare them for real-world discussions where they will have to take turns, express their opinions in front of others, and listen to the ideas of more than one person. Reading workshop is a great place to cultivate these conversations, but they can be incorporated into any part of the instructional day.

Big Idea: Ask and Answer Questions About Key Details

TRANSFORMING TEACHING	
Ask questions that are not dependent on the text- or illustrations-based evidence. Readers seldom revisit the text for answers or confirmation.	Create text- or illustration-dependent questions that compel the reader to revisit the text to find/confirm answers and cite evidence to support their answers. For example, "How do you know? What evidence does the author give us?"
Primarily ask literal questions that can easily be answered with or without the text.	Ask open-ended, higher-level questions to engage thoughtful debate and collaborative conversation that lead to deeper understanding of the text.
Read informational texts once to learn about the main idea and details.	Select excerpts of texts to closely read for a variety of reasons.

Inquiry Experience: Read Closely for Different Purposes

TARGETS

- I can better understand text by reading it closely.
- I can quote accurately from a text to support my thinking about it.
- I can use text evidence to support my thinking about a text.

PREPARATION

- Select a text and identify a part or passage(s) that can be read closely. If you want students to annotate text, make multiple copies so that each student can have a copy of what is being read.
- Create text-dependent questions, ideally in collaboration with colleagues as a professional development activity. See box on page 101 for different types of questions you might ask after reading the selected text.

Types of Text-Dependent Questions
for 3–5 Readers

The following question types were identified by Fisher & Frey (2012):

❈ *General Understandings:* General understanding questions may ask the reader to retell parts of the story or identify the main idea in an informational text. These questions focus on literal comprehension and help students focus on what's most important in the text.

❈ *Key Details:* Readers locate key details and ideas within the text by asking *who, what, where, when, why,* and *how.* In informational text, these details enable the reader to make literal meaning from the text. In fictional text, identifying the character, setting, problem, and solution create the framework for understanding how the story is being told.

❈ *Vocabulary and Text Structure:* Vocabulary queries ask readers to clarify unknown words and multiple-meaning words by using word clues (prefixes, suffixes, root words) and/or sentence-level context clues. In literature, ask students to identify words in the text that show feelings or emotions. In informational text, encourage students to identify unknown words and examine the context in which the words are presented. Clues to the meaning of these words may also appear in illustrations or other text features.

❈ *Author's Purpose:* Figuring out the author's purpose helps the reader identify the person telling a story and gives clues as to what the author wants the reader to remember or do after reading the text. Questions such as, "What are you thinking about after reading the text?" "What do you think the author wanted you to think about after reading the text?" and "Why did the author write the text?" can be posed to readers of both fiction and informational text. Discuss reasons why authors might choose to write informational text such as a biography or article. This can lead to a great conversation about point of view and how it affects the reader's perspective.

❈ *Inferences:* Making inferences helps the reader to "read between the lines." Understanding what is implied in the text also requires the reader to understand what is explicitly stated in the text. Asking follow-up questions such as "Why do you think that happened?" gets the reader thinking beyond the literal ideas presented in texts.

❈ *Opinions, Arguments, and Intertextual Connections:* Helping readers think about how texts are interrelated helps them form opinions about what they have read and support those opinions with evidence from multiple texts.

EXPLANATION

In their book *Falling in Love With Close Reading: Lessons for Analyzing Texts—and Life* (2013), Christopher Lehman and Kate Roberts discuss how readers can begin to set their own purposes for close reading. This practice involves slowing down at key points to notice and name details about the text and the author's craft in order to understand the text more deeply. If we teach our readers to habitually stop and reread a portion of text, it becomes another valuable tool in their reading toolbox.

The goal of close-reading instruction is to help our readers become metacognitive about their reading and become independent readers who know when a sophisticated text needs a second, closer look. As with any new skill, close reading requires a great deal of modeling and practice, but we know that students will eventually be able to do it on their own with success and confidence.

What Is Close Reading?

* It is a habit that experienced, strategic readers employ when they want to understand a text more deeply.

* It involves making careful observations about a text and then making thoughtful interpretations about those observations.

* It involves rereading with a specific purpose or question, identified by the teacher or reader, that helps the reader better understand the text as a whole.

EXPERIENCE

Modeling and Demonstration

One of the keys to close reading is rereading a text multiple times. Before beginning a close-reading experience, stress to students that there will be places in the text when they will need to read closely to better understand it or to answer a text-dependent question. Remind them that this is what experienced readers do when they are having trouble comprehending or know that a particular section is very important. Talk with them about times when you have read closely for each of these reasons.

* Read aloud the text that you've chosen.

* Return to specific portions of the text to demonstrate close reading. Lehman and Roberts describe this process as reading the text through a "lens," focusing on specific types of details in order to look for patterns so as to better understand the text. For instance, you might prompt students to listen for details related to the main character during an important scene to better understand his or her actions.

* As they read, have students mark their copy of the text with a pencil or sticky notes to flag interesting or important details.

* Afterward, have students review their notes and think about the patterns they see and how those patterns help them better understand the text. Model this process the first time or two, then have students discuss their thinking with a partner or small group. Remind them to cite text evidence, including direct quotations, to support their ideas.

* Lastly, have students reflect on the process of close reading and how it helped them better understand the text. Ask students, "How has this process helped you as a reader to process this text?"

* Encourage students to use this strategy in their independent reading when they encounter a confusing part, an important scene, or a section that contains lots of detailed information.

Independent Practice and Application

Have students think about how they use close reading for their own purposes. During a conference, ask them to identify a time when they had to use close reading to better understand a portion of the text that was confusing, important, or dense. This is how you can begin to foster independence for your students with this important strategy.

Putting the Pieces Together Through Close Reading	Reading Fiction Closely for Character Details
1. Read for a purpose.	Choose specific details about the character: • How does the character act? • What does the character think about himself/herself and others? • What relationships does the character have with others? • How does the character "fit into"/interact with the setting of the story?
2. Use the details to find patterns.	• How do the details that I've collected fit together? • What do they tell me about the story?
3. Use the patterns to better understand the text.	Look at patterns to think about: • The main character's traits • The main character's relationships • The theme of the story

(Adapted from Lehman & Roberts, 2013)

Tried-and-True Fiction Texts for Close Reading

Title, Author	Brief Summary
Journey (Becker, 2013)	A girl travels to a magical land through a door that she drew with her red crayon. She finds herself ultimately a prisoner in a cage, but, with the help of a unique bird and her crayon, she makes a new friend with a blue crayon and they ride off on a tandem bicycle that they have drawn together.
Hermelin: The Detective Mouse (Grey, 2014)	Hermelin is a small white mouse who secretly helps the residents of Offley Street by solving the mysteries that are troubling their lives. When the grateful people decide to throw a party for their benefactor, they are shocked to learn that the detective is a mouse. He is banished to pest status until his own benefactor comes to save the day for him.

Title, Author	Brief Summary
The Invisible Boy (Ludwig, 2013)	Brian seems invisible to his classmates and even his teacher. One day a new boy, Justin, joins the class, and the other students begin to make fun of him because is different from them. Brian decides to befriend him by giving him a note letting him know that he is special. Justin appreciates this and begins to be friends with Brian. Other students notice this and begin to be friends with Brian, too. Now Brian isn't so invisible anymore.

Putting the Pieces Together Through Close Reading	Reading Informational Text Closely for Key Details
1. Read for a purpose.	Choose specific details to gather as information: • Facts or other important information • Descriptions of concepts, people, or events • Informational graphics or other text features
2. Use the details to find patterns.	• How does the evidence that I've gathered fit together?
3. Use the patterns to better understand the text.	Look at the patterns to think about: • The main idea of a whole text • The author's bias or point of view

(Adapted from Lehman & Roberts, 2013)

Tried-and-True Informational Texts for Close Reading

Title, Author	Brief Summary
Gravity (Chin, 2014)	A beautifully illustrated book explaining the concept of gravity. It illustrates what life is with and without gravity in our daily lives.
Me . . . Jane (McDonnell, 2011)	This is the story of Jane Goodall and the beginning of her fascination with animals. This book focuses on her childhood and how she was given a toy gorilla and became attached to it, and how that influenced her later life.
If: A Mind-Bending New Way of Looking at Big Ideas and Numbers (Smith, 2014)	A collection of complex mathematical and scientific concepts told in a way that makes them easier to think about for learners of all ages.

Some Examples of Questions to Get Readers Thinking About Text Evidence

✳ What in the text makes you think/say that? Can you show me evidence in the text to support your thinking?

✳ How do you know? Where in the text is evidence for your thinking?

✳ How did you come up with that idea? Where in the text did you get that idea?

✳ Who agrees or disagrees? How might you explain other interpretations of the text that differ from your own?

✳ Does anyone have any other ideas? Does the text open up your thinking to looking at the topic in a different way?

Inquiry Experience: Making Inferences

TARGETS

- I can think critically and make inferences from the text.
- I can support my ideas with evidence from the text.

PREPARATION

- Choose a literary or informational text to share (either a picture book, poem, or short passage). Identify two or three places where you can model making an inference. Select two or three more places where you can invite students to make inferences.

- Begin an anchor chart about inferences; see the sample at right.

EXPLANATION

Inferences are conclusions that readers make based on clues in the text. The goal of inferring is to figure out what the author is saying beyond the literal meaning of the words. Readers need to understand that when they are inferring, there may be more than one right answer to the question of "What do you think and why?" When students make inferences regarding their reading, they integrate their understanding of the text with previously read texts and background knowledge. When students do this in conjunction with collaborative conversations and complex texts, their thinking is elevated. This is a difficult skill for students, so we recommend repeated modeling and guided practice with increasingly complex texts throughout the year.

When Readers Infer They Do the Following:

✳ Think about what is happening right now in the text, rather than predicting what will happen next.

✳ Use their schema or background knowledge and clues from the text to "read between the lines."

✳ Answer questions that are not explicitly stated in the text.

✳ Confirm or change their inference as they gain more information from the text.

✳ Determine the big idea, central message, or theme of the text.

✳ Examine evidence from the illustrations and/or text to make insightful inferences.

✳ Deepen their comprehension.

Thinking Stems for Inferring

❋ I think that . . . because . . .

❋ I think . . . happened because . . .

❋ The character acted/ reacted . . . because . . .

❋ It could be that . . . because . . .

❋ This could mean . . . because . . .

❋ I'm inferring . . . because . . .

❋ I can conclude . . . because . . .

EXPERIENCE

Modeling, Demonstration, and Guided Practice

- Display the anchor chart you've created and introduce or review the concept of an inference.

- Introduce your read-aloud text and say something like, "Today we are going to look for ways that we infer what the author is telling us without his or her saying it in words. Let's look for ways that we can do this in the text that we are reading today." Stop during the read-aloud at the points you identified and think aloud as you make an inference, explaining how the inference is based on your experience and knowledge and discussing how it helps you better understand the text. You may choose to use a graphic organizer like the one below to record your thinking.

- Refer to the anchor chart as a reminder about what an inference is.

- Continue to read aloud, pausing at selected points to ask students to make inferences about the text. Students can share their thinking with a partner or write their ideas on sticky notes to add to the anchor chart. Guide students as they are thinking and sharing their thinking, noticing who might need some additional support in a conference.

Independent Practice and Application

As students become more proficient at making inferences in their independent reading, we give them some of the prompts like those above to write about in their reader's notebooks. As the year progresses, ask your readers to help you brainstorm other prompts to talk or write about. After some successful experiences with making inferences, they'll come up with many impressive ideas to add to your list!

Another option for having students record their inferences while reading is the graphic organizer at right. As teachers, we know how important it is to have a variety of tools at our fingertips to differentiate for a wide range of learners or to use when we model with our students. You may use the organizer when modeling during a whole-class read-aloud and then have students respond to the thinking stems using their reader's notebook with their independent reading book. We've found that this is a great way for students to capture their thinking about inferring.

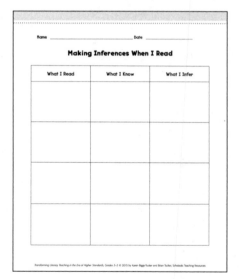

Big Idea: Consider Themes, Central Messages, and Morals

TRANSFORMING TEACHING	
Summarize basic story elements of text.	Summarize the basic story elements as well as infer the theme or central message of stories, dramas, or poems.
Select texts with predictable themes, such as friendship.	Select texts with richer, more relevant age-appropriate themes or central messages, such as bullying, homelessness, and special-needs children.
Read traditional tales from our culture.	Read traditional tales and versions of those tales from various cultures, introducing students to aspects of those cultures.

Inquiry Experience: Summarize Text

TARGETS

- I can summarize a text to understand its main idea and theme.
- I can include supporting details in my summary.

PREPARATION

- Gather both fiction and informational texts that can be used for summarizing practice. (Initially, use fiction texts with identifiable beginning-middle-end plots and informational texts that have clear text structures and organization and that lend themselves to modeling and practice by your students.)
- Chart paper/interactive whiteboard for teacher modeling

EXPLANATION

Summarizing fiction and informational texts is a useful way for students to identify and remember the important parts of a text. For fiction, students should name the story elements and identify key plot events. For informational text, students should state the main idea and report the key details that support it. The summarizing process requires readers to edit out much of the detail that they might have included in a retelling or recounting in earlier grades. The following experience models multiple strategies for summarizing that support students as they take the first step toward the ultimate goal of summarizing and inferring theme.

EXPERIENCE

Modeling, Demonstration, and Guided Practice

Model each strategy for summarizing listed on the chart on page 108 during a read-aloud or mini-lesson. After your demonstration, invite readers to try summarizing after a read-aloud, sharing with a partner for support. This gives you the opportunity to provide feedback and support to students who may need additional help with this skill.

Summarizing Fiction Text	Summarizing Informational Text
SOMEBODY, WANTED, BUT, SO Summarize events in the story by including the following: • **Somebody:** Character • **Wanted:** Character's goal or motivation • **But:** Problem(s) character faced or encountered • **So:** Solution that resolved the problem faced by the character *(Macon, Bewell, & Vogt, 1991)*	**K-W-L** • Prior to reading a passage, students generate what they already *Know* about the topic and ask questions about what they *Want* to know about the topic of the passage (K & W) • After reading the passage, students revisit their questions, writing what they have *Learned* from their reading (L) (Students can combine their background knowledge and the information learned from the text to write a paragraph summarizing their learning. Note: Students may change what they know based on information that they have read if their background knowledge is inaccurate or needs to be changed based on their reading.)
C.L.A.P.S. • **Character:** Name of the main character • **Location:** Setting • **Action:** Character's goal or motivation • **Problem:** Problem(s) faced by the character • **Solution:** How the character solved the problem in the story *(Fuhler & Walther, 2007)*	**WHO, WHAT, WHERE, WHEN, WHY, HOW?** • Who/what is the passage mainly about? (topic) • What is (are) the most important idea(s) presented about the topic? • When does this take place? • Where does this take place? • Why is the topic important? • How does this occur? (Students answer as many of these questions as possible based on the information in the text.)

Independent Practice and Application

Continue to provide opportunities for students to practice summarizing both fiction and informational texts. When you feel ready to release responsibility to your students, prompt and coach readers to practice independently. This should be done during conferences or during shared reading frequently throughout the year, and progressively with more complex texts.

Inquiry Experience: Determine Theme or Message

TARGET

I can infer the theme or central message of a text, poem, or play.

PREPARATION

• Choose texts, poems, or plays that are related to units of study or topics of interest to your students. See page 110 for some common themes found in children's literature, and the chart below for some books related to those themes. Select points in the text where you will pause and ask questions to help students identify details that pertain to the theme. Mark these points with sticky notes.

- Create an anchor chart with a kid-friendly definition of theme, such as the one below.

WHAT IS THEME?

- The author's message to the reader.
- A "life lesson" that the reader can apply to his/her own life.
- What the reader is pondering when finished with the text.
- It can often be summarized in a few words (like a bumper sticker or a refrigerator magnet).

SOME QUESTIONS THAT THE READER ASKS TO HELP DETERMINE THEME:

- Why did the character act the way that he/she did in the story?
- How did the character grow or change?
- What did the character learn through his/her experiences? How might I apply this to my own life?

Book Title	Possible Theme	Brief Summary	
Mr. Tiger Goes Wild (Brown, 2013)	Be yourself/ Don't be afraid to "change the world"	Mr. Tiger lives in a world of prim and proper gentlemen, but one day he has a wild idea. He decides he wants to be different, but being different isn't what everyone else does. What will Mr. Tiger do, and what will everyone else do when they see what Mr. Tiger has done?	
The Memory String (Bunting, 2000)	Treasure your memories and the memories of others/ Give new people in your life a chance to care about you	Laura keeps buttons on a memory string to help remind her of her mother. One day she loses a very special button from that string. Her stepmother, Jane, helps her and that helps Laura realize how much she cares for her.	
The Smallest Girl in the Smallest Grade (Roberts, 2014)	Be observant of life around you/Find your voice and stand up for what is right	Sally notices everything, even though no one notices her. One day she notices someone being bullied and she stands up for what is right. Her noticing has made a big difference in a very important situation.	

Book Title	Possible Theme	Brief Summary
The Can Man (Williams, 2010)	Understand the difference between your needs and wants/Helping those less fortunate	When Tim's parents can't afford to buy him a new skateboard for his birthday, he looks for ways to earn money. Along comes Mr. Peters, a homeless man dubbed "The Can Man" for collecting cans, which gives Tim an idea. Soon Tim discovers that he has taken away Mr. Peter's only source of income.

Some Themes Found in Children's Literature

* Choose kindness
* Cooperate with one another
* Celebrate diversity
* Stand up for what is right, even when it isn't easy
* Care for one another
* Always do your best
* Appreciate others
* Overcome adversity
* Accept yourself as you are

EXPLANATION

Authors of well-loved children's literature incorporate themes that leave readers thinking about big ideas. The theme brings together details about the character, setting, and plot that ultimately express the author's purpose. Guiding readers to uncover themes helps them better understand texts and appreciate the deeper meaning of what they read. Since this can be a challenging activity for young learners, we model the process of determining themes during read-alouds, using increasingly complex texts throughout the year.

EXPERIENCE

Modeling and Demonstration

Begin by displaying your anchor chart and introducing or reviewing the concept of theme. Then introduce the book and read it aloud, pausing at selected points to ask questions that will guide students to understand the theme; you'll find a sample read-aloud experience for theme below.

There are so many wonderful books that you can read to discuss theme with your students. Some of them we have listed on pages 109–110, and many more can be found on library shelves in our classrooms and libraries (and yours, too!). For the demonstration below, we'll use the book *Stand Straight, Ella Kate* (Klise, 2010), which shows how a young girl responds to the challenge of being taller than everyone else around her.

Sample of a read-aloud experience for theme

* "Today we're going to read a new book, *Stand Straight, Ella Kate*. As I read, I'm going to think about the characters, their actions, and the events in the story to try to understand what the theme of the story is. Remember, the theme of a story, poem, or play is the big idea or message the author wants us to understand. Sometimes the author tells us the theme in words; other times we have to infer it using clues. Sometimes we think of this as the 'me' message in the story, or the life lesson that the reader can take away from the text.

* "*Stand Straight, Ella Kate* is a true story about a girl who had a very interesting problem as she was growing up. She grew taller each year just like you, but something was different as she grew, and that presented a challenge for her. Let's read and see what her challenge might have been and how she responded to it. As we do that, let's think about it how we can apply the lesson that we learn from this book to our own lives."

- Read aloud the text, showing students the illustrations until the bottom of the page where it says, "'Stand straight, Ella Kate,' Mama said when she was fixing my hem. But when Mama wasn't looking, I hunched my back so I'd look smaller."

- Ask: "What was Ella Kate's challenge? How do you know? What was Mama's advice? What did she mean? How did Ella Kate respond? Why do you think she did that?" Allow time for students to respond and discuss.

- Continue reading until the bottom of the page where it says, "'I'll tell you what that girl is,' yelled a boy. 'She's a freak!' I ran off the stage in tears."

- Ask: "How is Ella Kate feeling? How do you know? Why is she feeling that way? What do you think she is going to do in response to this?" Allow time for students to respond and discuss.

- Then continue reading until the bottom of the page where it says, "'I believe I'll take that job,' I said."

- Ask: "What do you think of Ella Kate's decision? What do you think will happen next?" Allow time for students to respond and discuss.

- Read until the end of the book, then prompt students to consider the theme by asking questions such as: "What was Ella Kate's challenge? How did she respond to it? Did she follow her mother's advice of 'Stand straight, Ella Kate?' How do you know? What was the theme of the story? What was it that the author wanted us to think about after we were finished reading the story? How did we use what we knew about Ella Kate, her actions, and what happened in the story to help us better understand what the theme was? What can you learn from this book to apply to your own life?"

Guided Practice

Continue providing read-aloud experiences for your students related to theme. Initially, look for books with more obvious themes. As students become comfortable determining theme from text details, move on to more complex texts, which may have multiple themes or more subtle ones. Create a class anchor chart like the one on page 109 as readers gather their thinking and discuss their ideas as a class. Ask readers, "Who determines theme? The reader? The author? Both?" As readers think about how they interact with the text, they think about the meaning embedded in what they read, and it deepens their understanding of the text itself.

Independent Practice and Application

After your readers have had many opportunities to practice finding and discussing themes, encourage students to identify themes in their own independent reading books and write about them in their reader's notebooks. Sharing their reader's notebook entries at a reading conference will give you insight into their development as readers and will help you know the types of complex texts they are ready to tackle.

Big Idea: Describe Characters, Settings, Events to Discover Connections

TRANSFORMING TEACHING	
Focus on identifying character, setting, and events in the story.	Expand the reader's understanding of story elements to look at how characters respond to the setting and events.

Inquiry Experience: Explore How Characters React to Events and Settings (Fiction)

TARGET

I can explore how characters interact with other characters, the setting, and the events in the text.

PREPARATION

- Choose texts with characters responding to key events. These can be picture books or chapter books. We typically use picture books like the ones listed below.
- Enlarge the character-study graphic organizer (below right) for recording student thinking during the read-aloud experience.

Books With Engaging Characters, Settings, and Events

Title, Author	Brief Summary
Sam & Dave Dig a Hole (Barnett, 2014)	Sam and Dave are on a mission to find something spectacular, but it seems to always be just beyond their reach. They are determined and keep trying. How will their day end, and will they find their spectacular treasure?
The Matchbox Diary (Fleischman, 2013)	A young girl's great grandfather tells his immigration experience through matchboxes that he has saved throughout the years. The stories chronicle his life and bring them closer together.
The Dark (Snicket, 2013)	Laszlo is a young boy who is afraid of the dark. The "dark" keeps to itself in the basement, until one night when it comes into Laszlo's room, an adventure happens and Laszlo learns not to be afraid of the dark anymore.

EXPLANATION

To help readers understand how characters, setting, and events in a narrative come together to create a story, provide them with quality literature, complete with interesting characters who evolve based on the settings and events they encounter. Exploring the relationship between story elements helps deepen students' comprehension, especially as a text becomes more complex. Moreover, as readers begin to think about how characters respond to the events and experiences in stories, they gain a better understanding of how they can react and respond to the ever-changing world.

EXPERIENCE

Modeling and Demonstration

If students haven't had a lot of experience analyzing multiple characters at a time, you may want to start by analyzing how one character reacts to key events in the story and changes over time. Once students are comfortable describing the events and the character's response, you can analyze two or more characters at a time and begin to compare and contrast characters.

- Begin by saying something like, "We can learn a lot about a character by the way he or she responds to the events in a story—to a conflict, a problem, or even a new setting. To help us see what the characters in our story are like and how they change during the story, we're going to use a graphic organizer to chart our characters' responses to important events or new settings."

- Display and explain the character-study organizer.

- As you are reading the book aloud, invite the students to stop you when key events occur.

- Record each key event on the chart. Ask students to describe the character's response to the event. Jot students' ideas on the chart (see the sample chart below for *Peanut Butter and Jellyfish*, Krosoczka, 2014). If both characters experience the same event, record each character's response.

- When you've finished reading, think aloud as you review the chart, exploring how the characters are similar and different, and how they changed because of their experiences.

Reflection Questions

❋ Choose one event/response and describe how the characters responded to the event in the same way. Why do you think that happened?

❋ Choose one event/response and describe how the characters responded to the event in a different way. Why do you think that happened?

❋ Choose one (or both) of the characters. How has (have) the character(s) changed based on his or her experiences? Why do you think that has happened?

Guided Practice

Once students seem comfortable describing characters' responses, give them copies of the chart and have them complete it during a read-aloud. Allow time for students to talk with a partner as they record key events and characters' responses. When you finish the read-aloud, have readers look at their charts, reflect on their ideas, and turn and talk about the following questions:

- How are these characters the same/different?

- How do you know that? What details from the text support your thinking?

- How did the characters change/evolve because of their experiences? Why do you think that happened? How do you know that?

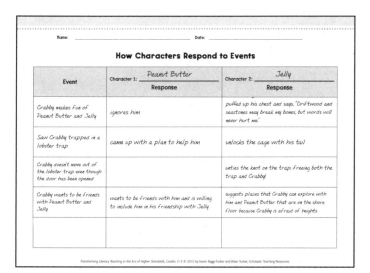

Independent Practice and Application

Once students are familiar with the graphic organizer and can use it to frame their thinking, duplicate the organizer and have students complete it for their own independent reading books. Then have students share their thinking with others in collaborative conversations or with you in a reading conference. These organizers can later be developed in reader's notebooks as written responses to self-selected books.

Inquiry Experience: Discover Relationships (Informational)

TARGET

I can explain the relationships that exist between two or more individuals, events, ideas, or concepts based on ideas found in informational texts.

PREPARATION

Gather resources related to your curriculum for students to read, discuss, and use to complete the organizer shown at right (available in online resources; see page 160), including the following:

- Articles

- Text sets

- Multimedia sources

EXPLANATION

To make your planning and teaching time more efficient, we suggest integrating this inquiry experience into your science or social studies instruction so that the work that students are doing is both authentic and relevant. This experience begins by having students read texts related to their content-area learning. Then they connect this learning to other texts to discover, analyze, and understand the relationships found in the informational texts that they have read.

EXPERIENCE

Modeling, Demonstration, and Guided Practice

- During a content-area lesson, demonstrate how you compare informational texts related to common topics in your curriculum. Show students how you discover connections among individuals, events, ideas, or concepts found in the texts.

- Engage in a shared inquiry with your students as you study people, places, events, and even scientific ideas that have influenced our lives as you explore informational texts throughout your curricular day.

- Choose two texts such as *Jack's Path of Courage: The Life of John F. Kennedy* (Rappaport, 2010) and *Moonshot: The Flight of Apollo 11* (Floca, 2009) to read with your students.

- Read-aloud each text separately using the graphic organizer shown above to record thinking throughout each text, recording important ideas related to the reading.

- When the organizer is completed, ask students the following questions to reflect on their learning:

  ❋ What did you learn from reading these two texts?

  ❋ How did this help you better understand the relationship between these people, places, or events?

Guided Practice

Have students take the information that they have learned from the reading of the texts and write a paragraph summarizing the connections made between the people and events presented in the texts. This encourages students to synthesize the learning from the texts and the big ideas in the graphic organizer into a written piece. Students may also want to generate follow-up questions for further research on sticky notes or in their reader's notebooks.

Independent Practice and Application

Encourage students to discover connections among individuals, events, ideas, and concepts that exist both in the curriculum and in their own lives. Invite them to discover those connections in their daily reading and share them with their classmates. Great conversation is sure to follow.

Big Idea: Understand Vivid Vocabulary

TRANSFORMING TEACHING	
Specific vocabulary is chosen and pre-taught by the teacher.	Students ask and answer questions about words that are puzzling to them and think about why the author chose to use those particular words in a piece of writing.
Students look up word meanings in a dictionary or glossary, copy the definition, and write a sentence using each particular word.	Students make connections between words to learn new words and ideas.
Books, poems, and short stories with literal language are used.	Texts filled with figurative language are used; students are invited to find words or phrases that evoke sensory images.
Grammar instruction is sometimes viewed as a separate subject. Grammar, conventions, and editing are taught by asking students to fix incorrect examples.	Grammar instruction is embedded in reading and writing workshop so students can directly apply their learning to their own speaking and writing. Grammar, conventions and editing are modeled by asking students to analyze well-crafted examples.

Inquiry Experience: Developing Word Knowledge

TARGET

I can use context clues to help solve unknown words when I read.

PREPARATION

- Select a curriculum-related topic.
- Choose a short text related to the selected topic.

- Make a class set of the Context Clues Chart (see below and online resources on page 160), and make or display an enlarged version of the chart for modeling.

EXPLANATION

As students develop their vocabularies, they need to be exposed to a wide variety of words both through listening to many texts and reading many books independently (Beck, McKeown, & Kucan, 2013). Providing time for students to choose unfamiliar words from their reading and then demonstrating how they can use context clues to figure out the meaning of the words builds their vocabularies.

EXPERIENCE

Context Clues

Context Clues help readers by giving them information in the text that they use together with their background knowledge to "solve" the meaning of unknown vocabulary words.

SOME CLUES THAT HELP READERS:

❋ *Definition:* the meaning of the word is given in the sentence with the new words

❋ *Example:* an example of the unknown word is given in the sentence (key words for the reader to look for are: *such as*, *for example*, and *including*)

❋ *Word Parts:* determine the meaning of the word by breaking down the word and examining its prefix, suffix, and root

❋ *Synonyms/Antonyms:* words related to the new words are presented in the sentence and may have similar or opposite meanings

Modeling and Demonstration

- After reading the text aloud together, identify several words that may be new from the passage.

- Distribute copies of the Context Clues chart to students, and display your enlarged copy. Write the first unknown word on the chart, and ask students to write it on their charts.

- Demonstrate for students how to use the strategies found in the chart at left to help determine the meanings of unknown words or to deepen the understanding of words that may already exist in their vocabularies. Model how to record context clues and the word's meaning on the chart; have students do the same.

- If there are not sufficient context clues in the sentence or surrounding text to determine meaning of the words, discuss with students other sources that they might use to determine word meanings (dictionaries, glossaries, and so on).

- Continue the process until students have found the meanings for all the new words in the text.

- Provide time for students to share their word charts with partners.

Guided Practice

Students may need additional support and practice in texts at their instructional reading level in a small group or during conference time. Then, you can give guidance in selecting words and using context clues to help the students discern the meaning of unknown words.

Independent Practice and Application

When you are ready for your students to work on their own, you may have your students do so in their independent reading books or informational texts.

Inquiry Experience: Understand Figurative Language

TARGET

I can understand figurative language, including similes, metaphors, and idioms.

PREPARATION

- Select a focus for instruction, the type(s) of figurative language you will explore (e.g., simile, metaphor, idiom)
- Gather a collection of texts that include examples of figurative language that match your instructional focus.
- Use chart paper or the interactive whiteboard for teacher modeling.

A Few Read-Aloud Texts With Figurative Language

Title, Author	Brief Summary
My Teacher Likes to Say (Brennan-Nelson, 2004)	A teacher's story with idioms, proverbs, and clichés that are often heard in the classroom and school setting.
Aunt Ant Leaves Through the Leaves (Coffelt, 2012)	A narrative story containing a variety of homonyms and homophones that are entertaining to readers of all ages.
Crazy Like a Fox: A Simile Story (Leedy, 2008)	Rufus the Fox is heading for a trip across the meadow and taking some of his favorite simile's along. This book explains the meaning of similes and presents a variety of them throughout the story.
You're Toast and Other Metaphors We Adore (Loewen, 2011)	A book filled with a variety of metaphors embedded in an engaging story about characters who experience the metaphors themselves.
It Figures! Fun Figures of Speech (Terban, 1993)	Introduces readers to the six common figures of speech—metaphor, simile, onomatopoeia, personification, alliteration, and hyperbole.
In a Pickle and Other Funny Idioms (Terban, 1983)	A collection of idioms with matching illustrations and explanations.

EXPLANATION

Readers need an understanding of the nuances of language. Children learn early on that many words have more than one meaning, and that some phrases don't mean what they say literally. Identifying and discussing examples of different types of figurative language—including similes, metaphors, and idioms—is a wonderful way to introduce students to figurative language. Depending on your students, you may want to introduce one type of figurative language at a time and work up to exploring multiple types in a single text.

EXPERIENCE

Read aloud your selected text(s), pausing to discuss examples of the type of figurative language under study. As you discuss the examples, provide students with the vocabulary to name the figure of speech along with a kid-friendly definition. Compare the literal meaning of the words to their figurative meaning, and discuss why writers use that type of language. Guide students to understand that figurative language adds interest and can create images that bring the writing to life or help the reader see something in a new way.

Sample of a read-aloud experience for idioms

This example is for teaching idioms, an important focus for intermediate students. The Amelia Bedelia books are some of the most timeless mentor texts for idiom instruction. The original *Amelia Bedelia* recently celebrated its 50th birthday with an edition that included some back matter on the creation of the book itself (Parish, 2013).

Modeling and Demonstration

- Introduce or review the definition of an idiom. Illustrate by giving some familiar examples, e.g., *It's raining cats and dogs; The test was a piece of cake.*

- Over the course of one or more read-aloud sessions, read several of the Amelia Bedelia books or other titles containing idioms.

- When you read an idiom, pause to discuss both its literal and figurative meanings.

- Make an anchor chart of the idioms you find. Encourage students to contribute other idioms to the chart.

Guided Practice

- Have students choose a favorite idiom from the ones they've just heard, then illustrate the literal and figurative meaning of the phrases.

- Share and discuss the illustrated idioms.

Independent Practice and Application

- Encourage students to look for figurative language in their independent reading. They can keep a list of these words and phrases in their reader's or writer's notebooks. You may choose to have students categorize their examples by type.

- Provide opportunities for students to share the figurative language they have found; encourage them to add shared examples to their lists.

- Invite them to use the figurative language that they have collected in their daily writing. Remind your learners how writers use figurative language to help make their writing more interesting.

Big Idea: Notice Text Structures

TRANSFORMING TEACHING	
Ask students to identify whether a text is fiction or nonfiction and/or identify the characteristics of fiction or nonfiction text.	Help students recognize the differences between fiction and informational text and the different ways that authors present information to readers. Students then apply these strategies to their own writing.

Inquiry Experience: Compare and Contrast Fiction Text Types

TARGETS

- I can explain how parts of a fiction text fit together.
- I can use what I've learned to help me understand fiction texts.

PREPARATION

- Select a variety of text types for students to compare and contrast, such as stories, novels, and plays.
- Use chart paper or an interactive whiteboard to record student thinking on fiction text types.

EXPLANATION

While most fiction contains the standard story elements—character, setting, plot, conflict, solution—different types have different structural features. An understanding of text structure enables students to firmly grasp how chapters, stanzas, and scenes work together to communicate the author's message, theme, or big idea. It helps them comprehend what they read better, and it gets them thinking about how to create texts of their own that adhere to the same structure.

EXPERIENCE

Modeling, Demonstration, and Guided Practice

- Introduce or review the idea of text structure and tell students you'll be exploring different types of structures found in fiction. Create and show students the anchor chart on which you'll be collecting notes about text structure.

- Over the course of several sessions, read aloud fiction texts of various types, such as those found in the box at right. After you finish with a particular type, ask students to name features they notice that are specific to that type; record their ideas on the chart.

- After you have read and discussed two or more types, invite students to compare and contrast their structural features. You may prompt students by asking questions such as these:
  - ❋ What is the difference between a picture book and a play? A poem and a novel? A novel and a picture book? (Remember to focus on the structure of the text.)
  - ❋ How are the pairs of text types similar? (Continue to focus the conversation on structure.)

Exploring Fiction Text Types

Most fiction texts have a narrative structure and contain the familiar story elements: character, setting, plot, conflict, and resolution.

- ❋ *Picture books:* The story is told through both words and pictures, and sometimes only in pictures (wordless picture books).

- ❋ *Novels:* The story is told in longer form and divided into chapters; it may or may not contain illustrations.

- ❋ *Plays:* The story is divided into scenes and can be acted out on stage with or without props.

- ❋ *Short stories:* Short stories may be collected into a book, written by the same author or multiple authors.

- ❋ *Fables, folktales, fairy tales, and myths:* The stories were originally part of a culture's oral tradition, passed down through generations and finally written down. There are often many versions of the same story.

- ❋ *Poems:* The text is divided into stanzas; it may or may not rhyme.

- ❋ *Songs:* Lyrics are often similar to poems, and are usually written in stanza form.

* How does the structure of the text help tell the story?

* How does the author use the structure of the text to communicate?

* Why did the author choose the particular text type to tell this story to the reader? Do you think the story would be better or worse if the author had told it in a different way? Why? How would it be different if it were told in a different text type?

- Record student thinking on the anchor chart.

- Continue to compare/contrast text pairs of different text types, modeling and demonstrating how to understand how the texts are structured and how their structures help readers better comprehend what they read.

- When you have finished the demonstration and modeling and completed the anchor chart, type it up and duplicate it for students to place in their reader's notebook for future reference in both reading and writing.

Independent Practice and Application

Encourage students to identify text types they encounter in their daily reading. Then invite them to try experimenting with different text types in their daily writing.

Inquiry Experience: Compare and Contrast Informational Text Structures

TARGETS

- I can compare and contrast informational text structures.

- I can use what I've learned while reading nonfiction texts.

PREPARATION

- Gather examples of nonfiction texts that include the text structure(s) you wish to teach; see the list on page 121.

- Provide students with sticky notes to use to record their thinking.

- Use chart paper or an interactive whiteboard to record student thinking.

EXPLANATION

With the emphasis that is placed on informational text in the new standards, students are expected to be reading more nonfiction than ever before. As we present them with a variety of texts, we expose students to more text structures, helping to nurture an essential awareness they'll need in order to comprehend informational text effectively.

EXPERIENCE

Modeling and Demonstration

- Introduce students to the various informational text structures (see the chart on page 121). We usually share one structure and then give students a day or two for guided/independent practice before moving on to the next one.

- Provide examples of the target structure, noting its purpose and how each author has used it effectively to convey information and show relationships between ideas. Elicit student input and record ideas on an anchor chart, creating a resource you can later type up, copy, and distribute to students for future reference.

- After you've introduced and discussed several text structures, show two texts on the same topic but with different text structures. Ask your readers the following questions:

  ❋ What do you notice about the information in these two books? Is it similar?

  ❋ Even though the same information is being presented in each text, how is it communicated differently? Why might one author have chosen to use a particular text structure to communicate about a topic?

- Add new ideas to the anchor chart.

- On another day, show two books on different topics with different text structures. Ask your readers the following questions:

  ❋ What do you notice about these two books?

  ❋ Why do you think some authors choose to use certain text structures in some content areas and other structures in other content areas? For example, historians use timelines to communicate historical events and scientists use charts and tables to communicate data. Why might they as authors choose to do that?

  ❋ How do the text structures help writers of informational text communicate information to the reader more effectively? Why do you think that?

- Add new ideas to the anchor chart.

Guided Practice

- Have students reflect on the questions listed above as they compare and contrast how authors use different text structures in informational texts that you read with them in small groups.

- Encourage students to write their thinking on sticky notes or in their reader's notebooks to share with partners or the group. As they share, help them discover similarities and differences in their thinking about why writers choose to use particular structures.

- Provide additional opportunities to look at books on a variety of topics from different content areas to explore how text structures are employed across the disciplines.

- Continue to guide students' exploration and conversation as they make discoveries about text structures within these books.

- Students may also look at articles and multimedia resources to see how those authors use text structures to organize and communicate their information to readers.

Independent Practice and Application

- After readers have had many shared experiences comparing and contrasting informational text structures, you may release responsibility to them by having them explore text structures in content-area books that you have available, or even in their science or social studies textbooks.

Informational Text Structures

❋ *Descriptive:* Provides details describing a person, place, thing, or idea

❋ *Problem and Solution:* Gives information about a problem and explains one or more solutions

❋ *Compare and Contrast:* Discusses similarities and differences between people, things, concepts, or ideas

❋ *Cause and Effect:* Describes an event or several events and the events that follow as a result

❋ *Chronological:* Provides readers with a sequence of events or a list of steps in a procedure

- Invite students to begin to incorporate different text structures into their own informational writing as your provide opportunities for them to write on topics related to your content-area curriculum.

Big Idea: Consider Purposes and Points of View

TRANSFORMING TEACHING	
Students focus on comprehending the story or content, rather than considering point of view.	Students are guided to understand how point of view impacts how the story or content is communicated.

Inquiry Experience: Distinguish Perspective

TARGET

I can understand how the narrator's perspective may influence how the story or information is told.

PREPARATION

Select a variety of books that are told from multiple points of view to enable readers to understand the world from different perspectives.

Some of Our Favorite Titles With Varying Points of Views

Title, Author	Brief Summary
Papa Is a Poet: A Story About Robert Frost (Bober, 2013)	The life of Robert Frost told from the point of view of his oldest daughter, Lesley. From the time he was a child, Robert loved language. Although his family thought that he would be a baseball player, he followed his passion and became a writer.
Dog Days of School (DiPucchio, 2014)	Charlie thinks that his dog Norman has a better life that he does. Then one day, he makes a wish to be a dog and his life gets turned upside down!
Little Red Pen (Stevens, 2011)	Little Red Pen is trying to correct a pile of homework all by herself until she takes a tragic tumble into the trashcan! Who will come to her aid and rescue her?
This Is the Rope: A Story From the Great Migration (Woodson, 2013)	This is the story of a family's migration north told from the perspective of a rope and its journey starting in South Carolina. For three generations, the rope is passed down and has been used as a jump rope, to tie suitcases, and ends up at a family reunion where the original little girl is finally a grandmother.

EXPLANATION

Literature provides students an opportunity to see the world through a variety of "windows." Providing books featuring narrators with a wide range of experiences helps to broaden the perspective of your students. As you prepare lessons on point of view, keep in mind the different types of point of view (see chart at right). We like to create an anchor chart on point of view for students to keep in their reader's notebooks to reference in a group setting or during their individual reading.

EXPERIENCE

Modeling and Demonstration

- Introduce or review the concept of point of view, referring to the anchor chart describing the different types, if you've created one.

- Read aloud a title that has a narrator with a unique point of view. (For some of our favorites, see the list on page 122.) Stop occasionally, asking students who is telling the story. Ask them to support their thinking with evidence from the text.

- When you finish reading, continue the conversation about how the narrator's perspective influences how he or she tells the events of the story. Ask questions such as the following:

  ✽ Who is the narrator of the story? Is the narrator a first- or third-person narrator?

  ✽ Does the narrator tell the events of the story in a true or accurate way? How do you know?

  ✽ If the narrator is not accurate, why not? How does that affect your reading of the story?

  ✽ How does the narrator's perspective influence the way the story is told? Why might that happen?

  ✽ Do other characters view the same situation differently? How? Would they tell it the same way, or a different way?

Guided Practice

- During collaborative conversations about point of view, it is helpful to guide these discussions with the following questions:

  ✽ Who is the narrator? What point of view is the story being told from?

  ✽ Why did the author choose to have the narrator tell the story from this point of view?

  ✽ Does the narrator's point of view give the whole story or just his or her perspective?

  ✽ How is the story revealed through the narrator's point of view?

  ✽ How might the story be different if it were told from another character's point of view?

Independent Practice

- As students read, have them identify who is telling the story and whether the narrator is trustworthy. Remind them to support their thinking with text evidence.

- Next, encourage learners to experiment with writing from different points of view. As they experiment with different narrators in their own writing, support them with mentor texts and the ones they are reading independently.

Inquiry Experience: Observe History From Different Perspectives

TARGETS

- I can analyze events or topics from multiple points of view.
- I can note important similarities and differences between accounts of the same events or topics.

PREPARATION

- Select a historical event or curricular topic about which you can create a text set of books, articles, poems, and so on, that present the event or topic from different points of view. A sample text set presenting different points of view of Rosa Park's history-making bus ride appears below.
- Gather clipboards and sticky notes so that your entire class can participate in the inquiry experience together.
- Prepare chart paper to collect students' ideas.

Rosa Parks Text Set Representing Differing Points of View

Title, Author	Brief Summary
Rosa (Giovanni, 2007)	The story of the civil rights movement beginning with Rosa Parks and her refusal to give up her seat on the bus. It then continues to chronicle other events leading up the present day civil rights activists and how they were influence by Parks.
I Am Rosa Parks (Meltzer, 2014)	Rosa Parks story is told from the perspective of her as a child and notes how she will change the world in her future. Filled with a wide variety of facts and her famous bus ride.
If a Bus Could Talk (Ringgold, 1999)	The story of Rosa Parks and her famous bus ride told from the bus that she rode on that fateful day.

EXPLANATION

Authors of informational text bring their own perspective to the topic, and sometimes a certain bias creeps into the information they are presenting, much as a narrator's perspective can influence how a story is told. It is important to help our students understand how point of view affects how we experience informational writing, just as it does with fiction.

EXPERIENCE

Modeling, Demonstration, and Guided Practice

- After reading two books on the same topic written from different perspectives, ask your readers the following questions:

❋ What do you notice about information in these two books?

❋ Is it similar? If so, how? Give examples from the text.

❋ How is it communicated differently? Give examples from the text.

❋ Why might the authors have communicated the information differently?

• Have students turn and talk with a partner about each question and then share their thinking with the whole group. Remember to have them support their ideas with examples from the text.

Sample Collaborative Conversation

Partner 1: I noticed that, in both of these books, Rosa decided not to sit in the back of the bus. Her decision was not what she was supposed to do because that's where the African Americans were supposed to sit.

Partner 2: Me, too. Don't you think that was very brave of her? I remember in *If a Bus Could Talk,* where the bus was telling her story, that she actually went to jail because she did that.

Partner 1: I agree with you that she was brave. I remember that she went to jail, too. I also remember that Dr. King spoke about a boycott because of what Rosa did.

Partner 2: I remember in *I Am Rosa Parks* that what she did influenced many people to stand up for what they believed in, too. I bet that made her feel proud of doing what she did.

Partner 1: I think that was why the bus that she rode on was so proud to tell her story to the girl who rode on it because she had been a part of history, just like Rosa Parks.

Partner 2: I noticed that both of the books had the message that Rosa Parks changed history. I think that is what the authors want us to remember. Don't you think?

Partner 1: I agree. Thanks for sharing your thinking with me today.

Partner 2: You're welcome. Thanks for sharing your thinking, too.

• Have students record their thinking on sticky notes. Collect these notes on an anchor chart that you can add to as you compare and contrast the points of view in additional texts.

Independent Practice

As a follow-up activity, in their reader's/writer's notebooks, students can choose another point of view not presented in the texts and write about the event from that perspective. For example, we read a text where Rosa Parks' famous bus ride was told from the perspective of the bus that she rode on (*If A Bus Could Talk* (Ringgold, 1999)). How might another famous historical event told from a different point of view sound compared the traditional story that we know? For example, Betsy Ross making the American flag told from the perspective of her sewing kit or the Wright Brothers taking their first flight told from the perspective of the airplane. The possibilities are endless . . . . What other ideas can you and your students come up with based on science and social studies units that you are currently studying in your classroom? After students have written their pieces, have them consider the following questions about their stories:

• How is the story the same when it is being told from a different point of view?

• How is the story different when it is being told from a different point of view?

• What qualities does changing the perspective bring to the event?

Big Idea: Integrate Illustrations, Images, and Text Features With Text

TRANSFORMING TEACHING	
Focus more on the meaning of words and less on the interaction between the text and illustrations.	Balance a focus on the meaning of a text with building an awareness of how illustrations and other graphic elements affect its overall message.

Inquiry Experience: Use Text Features to Enhance Informational Text

TARGET

I can analyze how text features help me better understand informational text.

PREPARATION

- Gather a variety of informational texts featuring a variety of text features, including pictures with captions, graphs, charts, tables, and so on.

- Gather clipboards and sticky notes so that your entire class can participate in the inquiry experience at the same time.

- Prepare chart paper to collect student ideas.

EXPLANATION

Students can gain a wealth of knowledge by reading closely the text features of nonfiction texts and thinking about why the author has chosen to use those features. Making purposeful choices in your content-area text selections, you can expose your readers to a wide variety of features that they may then choose to incorporate into their on informational writing.

EXPERIENCE

Modeling and Demonstration

- Introduce the concept of text features to your students, referring to the anchor chart on page 127 which shows some of the text features that they may encounter.

- Distribute copies of an informational text that contains some of the features that you have introduced.

- Together, identify and discuss the purpose of each text feature in the piece. Alternatively, you can have pairs work collaboratively to mark text features with sticky notes and discuss the purpose of each feature before sharing with the whole class.

- After completing your exploration of the text features, ask your students the following questions:
  - ❋ How do text features help the reader navigate informational text?
  - ❋ How do text features help the reader better understand the information presented in the reading?
  - ❋ How might you incorporate text features in your own informational writing?

Some Common Text Features in Informational Text

Text Feature	Description & Purpose
CAPTION	words or phrases that tell more about photographs, illustrations, tables, diagrams, and so on
HEADING/SUB-HEADING	word or phrase that states what the section following is about; usually the main idea
CHART/GRAPH	presents information in a clear, visual way
PHOTOGRAPHS/ILLUSTRATIONS	visual representations of information
DIAGRAM	a labeled drawing
MAP	visual image of a geographic place
TABLE OF CONTENTS	list of the parts of a book in the order in which they will appear within the book; located in the front
INDEX	alphabetical listing of subjects; located in the back of the book
GLOSSARY	alphabetical listing of important words and definitions at the end of the text
TIMELINE	presents information in chronological order that may not be presented explicitly in the text
SIDEBAR	boxed off section containing interesting or important information

A Few of Our Favorite Informational Books With Interesting Text Features

Title, Author	Brief Summary	
The Story of Snow (Cassino, 2004)	A variety of questions about snow are answered in this beautifully illustrated book about a favorite winter topic, snow.	
Locomotive (Floca, 2006)	The story of the creation of the transcontinental railroad and its importance in the history of our country. Showing how people used the railway to travel from one coast to the other because of this railway system and the locomotive that moved on it, the book chronicles an important event in our nation's history.	
Chitchat: Celebrating the World's Languages (Isabella, 2013)	A guide to the languages of the world including oral, written, and sign languages. A celebration of the spoken word that unites all readers (and speakers) of language.	
The Story of Salt (Kurlansky, 2014)	Salt has played an important role in our world. From its scientific makeup to its role in civilizations, the book chronicles this necessary element in our daily lives.	

Independent Practice

Provide students with a copy of the chart above for their reader's notebooks so that they can continue to identify and discuss text features in their informational reading. Give students sticky notes to mark places where text features are used in the nonfiction books that they read in their independent reading and content-area books. Allow time for students to compare how, when, and why authors use these features to help readers better understand their information.

Inquiry Experience: Access Information From Multiple Sources

TARGET

I can draw information from multiple print and digital sources to answer questions and solve problems.

PREPARATION

- Find multiple print and digital sources of information for a topic that you are currently studying.
- Create your own T-chart to be used as a class anchor chart for later reference.

EXPLANATION

In this experience, students learn to close-read a variety of informational texts and digital media. This skill is especially important as students encounter nonfiction texts that require the use of different comprehension strategies based on varying structures and features. We are also helping students build background knowledge for content learning, exposing them to academic vocabulary, and nurturing the skills they will need in order to seek out information about self-selected topics on their own. Finally, the additional practice working with texts and multimedia information enhances students' ability to locate an answer quickly and solve problems efficiently, which improves their confidence.

EXPERIENCE

Modeling, Demonstration, and Guided Practice

- Share the print and digital sources you have gathered related to your topic.
- Have students generate questions related to the topic; record them on the T-chart. Guide students to brainstorm a wide range of questions.
- Model how to find an answer to a question. Think aloud as you consider what type of resource might contain the information you're looking for. Then demonstrate how you can preview an article, book, or Web resource to determine if it has information related to your question. Show students how to look at the table of contents, index, headings, links, highlighted words, and so on to determine a resource's relevance for a particular question.
- When you've found an answer, model how to record it in your own words in the second column of the T-chart. Be sure to record the source of the information. This is a good opportunity to teach or review paraphrasing or punctuating a direct quotation.
- Ask students to choose another question to research. Use students' suggestions to select and preview sources. When they find an answer, invite students to paraphrase the text and record the answer on the T-chart.
- Repeat the process a few more times as necessary. If you have enough materials for the group to share, students can work in pairs. Once several questions have been answered, review the

information that's been recorded on the chart. Talk with students to synthesize the information. Model writing a paragraph on the bottom of the chart that summarizes the learning.

- On another day, with another topic, begin the session by asking students to generate questions about the new topic; write them on a chart, leaving plenty of room to write the answers.

- Invite pairs to choose a question to research using the materials you have provided.

- After pairs have found answers, ask students to write their information next to their question. Color-code answers so it's easy to see what information came from each source.

- Review the entire chart, noting all the great information the class has discovered about the topic. Encourage students to reflect on the learning by talking with a partner and then synthesizing the information in a written paragraph in their reader's notebooks.

- Finally, have students share their synthesis paragraph with a small group. Invite students to reflect on the process of gathering information by asking the following questions:

  ❋ How did you gather information from multiple sources to help you learn about your topic?

  ❋ What were some of the differences between reading and gathering information from written and digital sources?

  ❋ How can you gather information from a source quickly to answer a question or solve a problem?

Independent Practice

Remind students of this process when they are collecting information for their independent research projects.

Big Idea: Compare and Contrast

TRANSFORMING TEACHING	
Students read familiar texts.	Students read familiar texts and less familiar ones to aid in comprehension and deepen their reading experience.

Inquiry Experience: Compare and Contrast Stories on Similar Themes/Topics

TARGET

I can compare and contrast stories that have similar themes and topics.

PREPARATION

Create text sets (3–5 fiction titles) on similar themes. (See a sample text set on friendship on page 130.)

EXPLANATION

As we guide students to think deeply about text and consider how authors present information, they build on their own knowledge from what they read. To compare and contrast fiction stories, students need to use what they know about story elements. They will build on this knowledge as they begin to think about how several texts treat a similar theme.

Sample Text Set on Friendship

Title, Author	Brief Summary
One Cool Friend (Buzzeo, 2012)	Elliot attends Family Fun Day at the aquarium and returns home with a new friend, a penguin! Their relationship goes unnoticed by Elliot's father as he is busy with other things.
The Story of Fish & Snail (Freedman, 2013)	Fish and Snail are friends. Fish ventures out of their fishbowl and brings back stories, but snail isn't comfortable doing so. One day he gets up the courage to do so . . . and his life is never the same again!
Two (Otoshi, 2014)	Two is best friends with One until Three comes along. Everything changes. Can One, Two, and Three all be friends at the same time?
The Crayon: A Colorful Tale About Friendship (Rickerty, 2014)	Two creatures begin with two crayons, but then they begin pulling out the other crayons in the box. Will they learn to share with each other?

EXPERIENCE

Modeling, Demonstration, and Guided Practice

- Review the concept of theme with students. The anchor chart in your students' readers' notebooks makes a good conversation starter. Over the course of several days, read each title in the text set, focusing your discussion on the theme and how each author develops it.

- After you've read the entire text set, invite students to compare and contrast how the themes were treated within it. Ask questions such as these:

  ❋ How are the themes similar? Is there one theme that applies to all the texts we read?

  ❋ What are the different ways each author presented the theme?

  ❋ As a reader, do you think about the theme in a different way because of how the author presented the idea?

Independent Practice

Refer your students to their Books I've Read list to look for books by different authors that share similar themes. Have students compare and contrast how different authors present themes in their books.

Inquiry Experience: Integrate Information From Several Texts on the Same Topic

TARGET

I can write or speak knowledgeably about information learned from multiple texts on the same topic.

PREPARATION

- Collect informational texts on a topic or subject in a curricular area that you are studying.
- Place students in partnerships or small groups of 3–4 students.

EXPLANATION

Integrating information from multiple texts requires students to read closely in order to gather important information. The goal of this inquiry experience is to provide students with a wide range of information to build their knowledge about the topic. The ability to share what they have learned through writing, speaking, or other media is good preparation for a lifetime of learning.

EXPERIENCE

Modeling, Demonstration, and Guided Practice

- Share the text set you have prepared with students on the content-area topic.

- Read each book aloud over the course of several sessions. Familiarize students with each text's structure and text features before you begin reading and set a purpose for each reading. Initially, a teacher-created text-dependent question will provide the focus, but the goal is for students to create their own questions as purposes for reading.

- After each reading, demonstrate how to record important information that addresses the purpose for reading. It may be helpful to revisit the chart on page 105 for asking questions, collecting information, and answering questions.

- Allow students time to read, research, and collect information about the content-area topic or one of their own choice. During the process, encourage them to discuss their information with peers.

- Provide support as needed by meeting with small groups and individuals based on your observations of students as they are working on locating information and answering their questions.

- When they have completed their research, encourage students to share their learning by writing an entry on a class blog. Taking information and sharing it with a public audience requires students to integrate their information from multiple sources so that they can teach others about what they have learned.

- Edublog and Kidblog are some sites that help you create blogs. They help you set up your blog so that only the students in your classroom can see the posts or enable your students and their families to see their learning. Some advantages for learning through blogging are listed at right.

Independent Practice

Once students have gone through this process, have them look for other topics, both within the curriculum and through multiple sources. After they have gathered information, provide opportunities for students to share their learning with others through speaking and writing.

Benefits of Blogging for Student Learners

* Focuses students on creating work using online tools

* Provides educational experiences and authentic audiences for student research

* Improves writing skills through authentic experiences with written communication

* Gives students a voice in a multimedia world

* Encourages collaboration within and beyond the classroom community

Big Idea: Search for Support in Informational Text

TRANSFORMING TEACHING	
Read informational texts once to learn the main idea and a few supporting details.	Closely read informational texts multiple times for a variety of reasons.

Inquiry Experience: Annotate Informational Text

TARGET

I can explain how an author uses reasons and evidence to support points in a text.

PREPARATION

Select a text and identify a part or passage for students to read closely for information. Make a copy of the text, or the portion of it, so each student will have a copy to write on during the lesson.

EXPLANATION

One aspect of literacy instruction that moves learners forward is close reading, or rereading for reasons. This strategy helps students slow down as they add new information to their knowledge base. This is especially important as they are accessing information in nonfiction text and identifying which facts are confirmed in their schema and which facts are new learning to be assimilated into their existing knowledge. Students need to begin taking responsibility for their own close reading and set their own purposes when reading informational text. Learning to annotate text is an important first step for students.

EXPERIENCE

Annotating text is one way that readers can record their thinking about text to help them refer back to it later for rereadings or discussions. Some suggested markings for intermediate learners that can get them started annotating their thinking as they read can be found in the chart at right and in the online resources (see page 160).

Modeling and Demonstration

- Introduce or review close reading as a strategy for slowing down at key points to comprehend more deeply.

- For the initial reading of the text, read for enjoyment and to get an understanding of the overall structure.

- Introduce each annotation mark, explaining what it is used for. Then talk through the process of using it on the text. Think out loud about why an idea is important or why it has sparked a question or an "aha."

- Have students reread the text carefully, using the text markings to annotate the text. Circulate as students work, supporting them as they read and annotate text.

- Have students share their annotations with a partner and discuss their understanding of the text based on the close reading and annotation. Students must support their thinking with evidence from the text.

- Finally, have students reflect on the process of annotation and how it helps them better understand informational text.

  ❋ How did annotating the text help you understand the text better?

  ❋ How did rereading the text help you focus on parts of the text that you had difficulty reading? What did you do when you reread a challenging part of the text?

  ❋ How does rereading informational text help you better understand it?

Guided Practice

Continue to provide practice with this strategy in small groups on individual conferences. Students may find it helpful to annotate text whether it is informational or literary. If they are unable to annotate directly on the written text, give students sticky notes to write their annotations on and refer to later. Remind students to refer to their annotations during discussions to help guide their collaborative conversations.

Independent Practice

Invite students to annotate their independent reading books to support them when they converse with other readers or when they have a reading conference with you.

Looking Back, Moving Forward

Guiding readers towards independence is an important role that we have as literacy teachers in the era of higher standards. We believe that as important as the achievement of the standards is fostering a love of reading in the students that we work with each and every day. Creating a community where students can have a choice in what they read, share their reading with others, and talk collaboratively about their thinking fosters a love of books. This passion for reading creates a confidence in readers that we, as experienced educators, know transfers into their ability to communicate effectively in writing. Next, we will take a look at how we take those engaged readers and move them along the literacy continuum to learn to write for a wide range of audiences and for a variety of purposes.

Chapter 7

Inquiry Experiences— Writing in Focus

Unlike Chapter 6, six of the inquiry experiences presented in this chapter take the form of teacher-guided writing units that move students through the stages of the gradual release model. Each of these inquiry experiences may last a few weeks.

- Write Our Own Opinions

- Conduct Research

- Write About Research

- Study, Write, and Present Historical People, Places, or Events

- Craft a Personal Narrative

- Write a Story

Go online to view a video on Inquiry Experiences— Writing in Action. See page 160 for details.

Whether you choose to repeat them during the course of the year will depend on the demands of your curriculum and the instructional needs of your students. Other less time-consuming inquiry experiences can be repeated based on your learning context and students' needs.

The sample schedule at right shows one way you might choose to organize these experiences across the year. The inquiry experiences are categorized according to whether they communicate opinions, convey information, or craft narratives.

Quarter 1	Quarter 2	Quarter 3	Quarter 4
Craft a Personal Narrative	Review a Book	Study, Write, and Present on Historical People, Places, and Events	Write a Story
Explore Opinions	Write Our Own Opinions	Write a Personal Narrative	Conduct Research and Write about Research
Conduct Research and Write About Research	Write a Poem	Write a Book Review	Compare Books and Movies

Big Idea: Communicate Opinions

TRANSFORMING TEACHING	
Lessons are focused more on narrative and expository writing.	Opinion-related conversations and writing opportunities occur throughout the year.

Inquiry Experience: Explore Opinions

TARGET

I can communicate my opinion through conversations and provide logical reasons and information to support my opinion.

PREPARATION

Think about places in your curriculum where you can weave opinion-related conversations and writing into the learning experiences of your students. Gather a book or two about topics that students will take a stand on in their conversations with one another.

Books That Lead to Opinion-Related Conversations or Writing Experiences

Title, Author	Summary	Idea for Follow-Up Opinion	
What's Your Favorite Animal? (Carle, 2014)	Fourteen children's book artists illustrate their favorite animals and why they love them the most.	• What is your favorite animal? Why? • What is your favorite _____? Remember to support your answer with reasons why it is your favorite.	

Title, Author	Summary	Idea for Follow-Up Opinion
The Day the Crayons Quit (Daywalt, 2013)	Duncan's crayons are on strike and have each written him a letter explaining why. What will he do to get them back?	• What would you say to Duncan's crayons to convince them to come back? • Which of Duncan's crayons is the most important? Why do you think that? • Which of your supplies is most important to you in your daily school day? Why? Remember to support your answer with reasons.
The Best Pet of All (LaRochelle, 2004)	A boy tries to convince his mother to get him a pet. He wants a dog, but ends up with a dragon instead. He finds that it may be the best pet of all!	• What do you think is the best pet? Why do you think that? • Try to convince your parents to do something or to let you do something. Remember to support your thinking with good reasons.
Which Would You Rather Be? (Steig, 2002)	Pairings of questions of which you'd rather be. Including . . . which would you rather be, a boy or girl?	Choose one of the pairs of questions from the book and choose a side. Support your position with reasons why you would make that choice.

EXPLANATION

Creating opportunities for opinion writing within your existing curriculum can be challenging, but these experiences are an important addition to your literacy instruction in light of the new standards. Having conversations about opinions is a great place to start.

EXPERIENCE

Modeling, Demonstration, and Guided Practice

Sharing mentor texts that showcase opinions is a great way to spark discussion about opinions. It provides model language for students to use as they discuss—and later write about—their own opinions.

- From the first day of school, look for opportunities to have conversations about the nature of opinions and demonstrate that opinions are not facts, but they are supported by facts. You may say something like, "I saw a wonderful movie over the weekend. It was a romantic comedy set in Europe, and the scenery was amazing! The story was sweet, but it was the music and the scenery that made me love it. What is the best movie you've seen lately? Why do you like it so much?" You can ask for students' opinions about a classroom activity, field trip, an assembly, and so on. Always prompt students to explain why they liked (or didn't like) something.

- Read aloud a book whose characters express divergent opinions, such as those above. Allow students time to discuss their own opinions on the topic.

Independent Practice and Application

Give students categories, such as favorite snack, television show, or season, and ask them to write two possible responses on index cards (e.g., chips/apple; *American Idol/The Voice*; fall/summer). Collect the cards, then invite pairs to draw one, state their opinion on the topic and explain their preferences. The cards are also useful as topics for quick-writes in writer's notebooks when students begin writing about their opinions.

Inquiry Experience: Write Our Own Opinions

TARGET

I can communicate my opinion through writing and provide logical reasons and information to support my opinion.

PREPARATION

Gather samples of opinion pieces to share with your students. Look for editorials, persuasive letters, or speeches on topics that matter to them.

EXPLANATION

Writing an opinion piece is different from persuasive writing. Persuasive writing entails establishing the writer's credibility and appealing to readers' interests, beliefs, emotions, or character in order to persuade the reader to adopt the writer's position or to take action. In opinion writing, the writer seeks to clearly express an opinion based upon logical reasoning. Opinion writing is a first step toward the evidence-based persuasive arguments that students will write in later grades.

Modeling, Demonstration, and Guided Practice

- Share and analyze well-written opinion pieces on a variety of topics with students.

- Discuss the characteristics of a well-crafted opinion piece; make an anchor chart to record characteristics such as the following:

    ❊ Clear purpose and well-defined audience

    ❊ Opening that hooks the reader

    ❊ Opinion stated in a bold and memorable way

    ❊ Opinion supported with reasons and examples

    ❊ Transition words to make it read smoothly

    ❊ Closing that leaves the reader thinking about the opinion

- On another day, model writing an opinion piece and have your students create their own along with you.

    ❊ Choose a topic and discuss it with students, arriving at an opinion to write about in your model. Sample topics include, *What was your favorite book that you read this quarter? What did you think about this morning's assembly? Should parents help with homework?* Note: Not everyone has to agree, but for the purpose of shared writing, choose an opinion. Remind students that they will have an opportunity to share their own opinions when they write independently.

    ❊ Determine the audience for whom you will be writing and decide on the voice you will use. For example, if the class is writing about a favorite book, the audience could be another class in the same grade, and the voice could be friendly and enthusiastic. This is a great opportunity for a mini-lesson on voice and its importance in writing.

    ❊ Share several leads with students from the mentor texts you have gathered and discuss how writers grab readers' attention in a variety of ways, from asking questions to telling stories (see a list of types of leads on page 138). Create a lead that hooks your readers by getting them interested in your topic and what you have to say about it.

Transition Words and Phrases That Writers Use

* First
* Next
* Then
* For example
* In addition
* For instance
* However
* Therefore
* Lastly
* In summary
* In conclusion
* Finally

* Demonstrate how to craft an opinion statement that is clear, bold, and memorable. Make sure that your students understand how important the opening is to the overall piece.

* After you've written your lead, invite students to write leads of their own on the same topic, trying out one of the hooks from the mentor texts you've discussed. Have students share their leads with a partner or small group.

* On another day, discuss the importance of supporting your opinion with reasons, examples, and evidence. Based on your students' needs, determine if you will write one or more supporting paragraphs and plan accordingly. Demonstrate how you brainstorm lots of ideas and then organize them prior to writing your paragraph(s), grouping related ideas together, adding specific details, and crossing out ones that don't quite fit. Discuss how all the details in one paragraph should support one main idea.

* Model writing a paragraph from your details, thinking aloud as you put the details in order and expand on your ideas in sentences. Once you have written a body paragraph (or more), have students write their own, using the strategies you modeled. Remind them of the importance of supporting their opinion with evidence.

* On another day, show your students how to craft an effective closing that summarizes the opinion. A good closing leaves the reader thinking about the opinion and supporting reasons. Invite students to write their own closings.

* When you have completed the shared writing piece together, students will also have a completed piece. This will be a great model that they can use as they begin their own independent opinion writing.

Ways to Hook Your Readers

* *Amazing Fact:* Start with a fact about your topic that draws your reader in because it is surprising or amazing.

* *Question to Consider:* Ask a question to get your reader thinking about your topic.

* *Famous Quote:* Begin with a quote by an expert on your topic or a famous person to pique a reader's interest.

* *Creative Description:* Use vivid language to describe a person, place, or thing.

* *Personal Opinion:* State your opinion about the topic before presenting evidence.

* *Startling Statistic:* Shock your readers with an alarming or unexpected statistic to get them thinking about your topic.

* *Sound (onomatopoeia):* Begin with a sound related to your topic to get the attention of your audience.

Independent Practice and Application

- Invite students to choose topics that they have opinions about and write their own pieces, based on the shared writing model.

- Provide opportunities for students to read their opinion pieces aloud so they can hear the sound of their individual writing voice in their piece—it's important! Then invite them to revise based on feedback from peers or their own reflections after sharing.

- Look for authentic audiences in the school and local communities with whom students can share their opinion writing.

Inquiry Experience: Review a Book

TARGETS

- I can state and support my opinion about a book in a book review.

- I can provide logically ordered reasons that are supported by facts and details.

- I can recommend books to other readers in my book review.

PREPARATION

- Collect samples of well-written book reviews.

- Discuss the purpose of book reviews and how readers often get ideas for their reading from other trusted readers or well-written book reviews recommending great books.

EXPLANATION

While rereading two influential professional books, *Writing Essentials* (Routman, 2004) and *Reading in the Wild* (Miller & Kelley, 2013), we were reminded of how valuable it is to have students recommend books to one another through book reviews. Creating opportunities for students to share their recommendations moves the responsibility of recommending titles to the classroom community as a whole. Teaching students how to write book reviews is a logical step in opinion writing because it extends the work we have been doing through conversations and opinion pieces. It also provides a record of each student's book suggestions, and students can reference the collection of reviews when looking for something to read.

EXPERIENCE

Modeling, Demonstration, and Guided Practice

- Choose a book that you and your students have read and enjoyed together.

- Review the characteristics of opinion writing with your students. Make the connection that a book review can convince readers to take action and pick up the book being written about, so writers must support their opinion with examples of what makes it a great read. Discuss the Steps to Writing a Great Book Review chart, shown on page 140, noting the similarities to the anchor chart you created for the previous experience.

To infuse voice in your writing, be sure to:

❋ Know the audience you're writing for.

❋ Use language that brings the topic to life in a way that engages your reader.

❋ Give the reader a sense of the person you are behind your words.

❋ Create a connection between you, your words, and your reader.

Steps to Writing a Great Book Review

❋ *Hook your reader.* Start with a lead that grabs your reader's attention.

❋ *Introduce the book.* Include its title and author, and tell a little about the book. (Remember not to give away too much—especially the ending!)

❋ *State your opinion of the book.* What did you like, or not like, about it?

❋ *Explain your reasons.* Support each of your reasons, with evidence from the text if possible.

❋ *Recommend the book to others.* What kind of reader might enjoy this book?

- In a shared-writing format, collaborate with your students to write the introduction to your book review. Remember to include a hook that will make your reader want to keep reading.

- Model how to use transitional words and phrases to add reasons for your recommendation.

- Think aloud about who might like this book and why. Include information about the genre, characters, and other details that might interest the reader you hope to persuade.

- Conclude your piece with a final opinion and a creative way to leave your reader wanting to add the book to his or her Someday List!

Independent Practice and Application

- Have students create their own book reviews, referring to the Steps to Writing a Great Book Review chart and your shared example.

- Have students post completed reviews on a bulletin board in a public place in school so others can see their recommendations.

- As a challenge, have students write a review of a book that they did not enjoy reading.

Inquiry Experience: Compare Books and Movies

TARGETS

- I can state and support my opinion.
- I can provide logically ordered reasons supported by facts and details.

PREPARATION

Select a read-aloud book with an accompanying short animated film (not a full-length feature), such as *The Snowman* (Briggs, 1978), *The Lorax* (Seuss, 1971), or the Magic School Bus series by Joanna Cole. Many of the older animated movie versions are available online or at your public library.

EXPLANATION

This experience will provide students with the opportunity to gather evidence from both textual and digital sources. Students naturally compare the book and movie versions of a story. As more and more books are made into movies, the number of choices available to students continues to grow. It can be interesting to discuss the effect of reading a book before seeing the movie, or vice versa, on how one experiences a story.

EXPERIENCE

Modeling, Demonstration, and Guided Practice

- After reading the book aloud and viewing the movie, ask, "Which version did you prefer and why?" Come to a consensus with your students about which opinion to express in the piece.

- As a class, review the characteristics of opinion writing.

- In a shared-writing format, create an opinion piece stating the consensus opinion and supporting it with examples from both the book and the movie.

- As you and your students reflect on your viewing, think about the film's visual elements and its music. Consider how events in the movie differed from the book, and note your overall experience of the book and movie. These are important details to include as supports for your preferences.

Remind students how important a good lead and a quality closing are to engaging your readers and leaving them remembering what you said.

Independent Practice and Application

- Encourage students to think of other familiar books that were turned into movies and write reviews of them to share with peers or other audiences.

- Reflect on this inquiry experience with your learners by asking questions such as the following:

  ❋ Are these experiences the same?

  ❋ Is the book always better than the movie? Is the movie always better than the book?

  ❋ Should you read the book before seeing the movie?

Big Idea: Convey Information

TRANSFORMING TEACHING	
Write informational pieces using traditional print sources of information.	Write informational pieces by gathering information from books, digital, and primary source documents.

Inquiry Experience: Conduct Research

TARGETS

- I can conduct research using several sources for a variety of purposes.

- I can communicate my research information to others through collaborative conversations.

PREPARATION

- Choose a content area that you would like students to investigate.

- Gather a variety of informational books, digital texts, and other resources at a variety of reading levels.

- Prepare chart paper or an interactive whiteboard to model brainstorming topics, note-taking, citing sources, choosing vocabulary, and so on.

EXPLANATION

In *Energize Research Reading and Writing: Fresh Strategies to Spark Interest, Develop Independence, and Meet Key Common Core Standards*, Christopher Lehman (2012) confirms that research skills are essential for our students, but he stresses that they are not easy to master. Research relies on asking questions, and the ability to ask questions is a vital skill for our students as citizens in a democracy. Giving them the tools to find the answers to their questions is an important component of our literacy and content-area instruction. The research cycle generally lasts for one or two weeks, but be sure to provide students with research opportunities throughout the year in various content areas—letting them make choices within the process whenever possible.

EXPERIENCE

Lehman offers teachers a roadmap to make research instruction manageable within the instructional day and to empower students with choices in their learning. We know how much having a say in what they read and learn about motivates our students to continue working, even when the going gets tough.

Day 1—Choose topics.

- During a guided-writing experience, brainstorm with students a list of topics related to the focus content area. Encourage students to think about how much information they know about each topic ("a little," "a lot," or "just right") so they can gauge how challenging the research process may be.

- Identify a topic that you will use to model the research process, thinking aloud about why you chose that topic over others. Record this topic on a piece of chart paper and indicate that no one else may choose this topic.

- Invite students to choose their own topics related to the content-area focus. Circulate and discuss with each student the topic he or she has selected and the thinking behind the choice.

Day 2—Identify questions to guide research.

- Refer to the topic you chose on Day 1. Model for students how to ask questions related to the topic to guide research. These questions should be of genuine interest to your students and should get at important ideas and information. For example, *Why are there three branches of government? How did the geography of our state affect its growth and development?*

- Discuss the difference between thick and thin questions. (See chart above, which might be displayed in your classroom and/or in writer's notebooks as a reference during the research process.)

- Encourage students to develop three to five thick questions for their topic. Circulate and provide support as they generate questions. Have students number their questions.

Days 3–7

Your students' needs and interests will determine how much modeling they need and how much time you devote to the research process.

Choose sources for note-taking.

- During a shared reading experience, gather sources for the selected topic. Model how you locate a source to help you answer your questions. Demonstrate how to use the table of contents, index, heading, bold words, and other text features to help answer a specific question.

Take notes with purpose.

- Demonstrate how to take notes that capture the main idea and key details of a text. Notes can take the form of either words or drawings. Some strategies for effective note taking are offered on page 144.

- Draw students' attention to the text features in the informational text as models for organizing their note-taking. Students can be creative in how they take notes, using charts, graphs, Venn diagrams, and so on to organize their thinking.

- As you take notes, indicate which question the notes relate to by writing the number of the question near each note.

- Model for students how to cite sources. Crediting source information can be as easy as writing the title and the author of a book, or it might also include copyright date, publisher, and city of publication for print sources and website information for electronic sources. Some online resources for information on proper citation of sources are Easybib, BibMe, and Purdue OWL.

Invite students to practice.

- Form groups of students who have chosen similar topics. Work with students to identify sources that will be most useful to them through the research process. Support students as they begin to navigate sources and look for materials that will help them answer their research questions.

- Remind students of the various note-taking strategies you have modeled and support them as they take notes from their sources. Ensure that they cite sources as they take notes.

- At the beginning of subsequent research sessions, have students reread their notes, thinking about the information they have already gathered and

---

Types of Sources to Use When Researching a Topic

PRINT RESOURCES:

❋ Books
  - *Single-topic book*—contains information about only one topic; may be more specific and thorough regarding topic
  - *Multi-topic book*—contains information about multiple topics related to a theme; because it has a variety of topics, it may have less information than a single-topic book

❋ *Periodicals/articles*—related to a variety of topics, can be more specific, and are published monthly, quarterly, etc., so information may be more current

❋ *Encyclopedia*—covers a wide variety of topics; each topic written by an author with expertise on the topic; short, concise text

ELECTRONIC RESOURCES:

❋ *Websites*—current and accessible, but must assess reliability before accepting information as factual

❋ *Apps for Tablets*—wide variety on a range of topics

❋ *YouTube or other online video streaming*—great resource as an alternative to reading text; resources from a variety of experts sharing their expertise on range of topics

Questions to Guide Collaborative "Teaching" Conversations

❀ What did you learn about your topic that you thought was most important for someone to know?

❀ What was the best source that you would recommend to someone interested in researching the topic?

❀ If you were writing a resource text for researchers studying your topic, what information do you think would be important to include?

❀ What advice would you give a novice researcher about the research process?

Strategies for Effective Note-Taking

READ, COVER, WRITE, AND REREAD

❀ Choose a short part of the text to read (usually 1–2 paragraphs).

❀ Read the passage carefully, thinking about the big ideas it contains.

❀ Cover the text and write down what you remember from the reading.

❀ Reread the text and what you have written.

❀ Ask yourself: *Does what I have written match what the text says?*

❀ Repeat for each section of text until completed.

READ, COVER, SKETCH, AND REREAD

❀ Choose a short part of the text to read (usually 1–2 paragraphs).

❀ Read the passage carefully, thinking about the visual images that the author's words create for the reader.

❀ Cover the text and sketch what you have visualized from the reading.

❀ Reread the text and look at your sketch.

❀ Ask yourself: *Does what I have sketched match what I visualized while I was reading the text?*

❀ Repeat for each section of the text until completed.

· ·

what information they still need to collect. Assure them that they will likely think of more questions during their research, and that this is both normal and beneficial to their learning. These new questions can simply be added to the list they've already started.

Days 8–9—Gather domain-specific vocabulary

❀ During a guided-writing experience, demonstrate for students how to keep a list of important words related to their topic.

❀ Choose three to five words from the sources you've used that are key words your reader needs to understand about the topic.

❀ Model how to write definitions for these words.

Day 10—Teach others about research through collaborative conversations.

❀ Demonstrate for students with another adult or student how to "teach" through a collaborative conversation. (See above for guidelines for collaborative conversations.)

❀ Remind students that the purpose of research is to help them learn about a topic and help them become "experts."

❀ Encourage students to communicate their discoveries about their individual topics through conversations about what they have learned.

Inquiry Experience: Write About Research

TARGETS

- I can conduct research for a variety of purposes, using several sources.
- I can communicate my research information to others through writing.

PREPARATION

- Gather class-created research notes from the previous experience.
- Collect mentor texts that showcase high-quality, creative informational writing, especially introductions and conclusions.
- Prepare chart paper or interactive whiteboard to model research writing.

EXPLANATION

Students need to be able to communicate their research both by speaking about it and through their writing.

EXPERIENCE

Modeling and Demonstration

Exploring the Genre

As you read and discuss the mentor texts, ask students to identify the qualities of informational writing and create an anchor chart. Discuss how research notes, much like those the students created in the previous inquiry experience, provided the starting point for these writers. Guide students to identify specific elements of craft and structure that they can incorporate into their own research as they transform their notes into a piece of informational writing.

Writing an Informational/Explanatory Body Paragraph

- Begin writing your class research text together. We like to begin writing the body paragraphs first because they often make the most sense to our writers, especially reluctant ones.
- Review the notes you took during the previous inquiry experience. Review your questions and the information you gathered to answer them, and determine a topic for your first paragraph. This is often the answer to the first question.
- Scan your notes for all the information related to the topic of the paragraph. (If you numbered your questions and coded your notes, this process is much simpler!) Think aloud as you read through your notes, identifying the big ideas and key details. Then craft a topic sentence that expresses the main idea of the paragraph.
- Explain that the sentences in the body paragraph share details about the big idea introduced in the topic sentence. Organize the key details you identified in a sequence that tells more about the topic sentence, then write meaningful sentences about the details.
- Highlight how you use transition words to link your ideas together. Refer to the list on page 138 that you have posted in your room on an anchor chart.

- If you are writing more than one paragraph, point out that transition words can be used not only between sentences within a paragraph, but also to connect one paragraph to another. An alternate way of transitioning between paragraphs is to connect the idea from the current paragraph with the main idea that you will discuss in the next one.

- Model writing two or three paragraphs, depending on your students' needs.

Writing an Informational/Explanatory Introduction

- Refer to the mentor texts you have shared and jot down some of the beginning lines of each book on a sticky note, interactive whiteboard, or chart paper.

- Discuss with your students what you notice about the beginnings of these texts. Refer to the types of hooks discussed during the opinion-writing experience (see page 138).

  ❋ Do the leads in the mentor texts fall into any of these categories? Why might writers of informational texts use these leads to engage their readers?

  ❋ How might you use these leads to grab your audience and make them want to keep reading about your research?

- Create several sample openings for the shared-research piece and have students choose which one they like best and explain why they think it is most effective in hooking the reader.

- Continue writing the introduction by previewing the information in the body text. (We usually have students write one sentence for each topic.) Remind students to use transition words within the introduction paragraph.

- End the introduction with a sentence that transitions the reader to the first body paragraph.

Writing an Informational/Explanatory Conclusion

- Return to the mentor texts and look at the last sentence or two. Jot them down on sticky notes, an interactive whiteboard, or chart paper.

- Discuss how authors close a piece of informational text and sum it up in a creative way.

  ❋ How do authors effectively close their writing?

  ❋ Do the closings in the mentor texts look or sound at all like the introductions? How?

  ❋ How might you use these kinds of closings in your writing to engage your readers and leave them thinking about your research after reading it?

- Create several effective closings based on the samples from your mentor text. Then have students choose which one they like best and explain why they think it is the most effective way of engaging readers.

Polish and Share

- Put the shared writing in its correct order, with introduction, body paragraphs, and conclusion.

- Read aloud together, revising and editing as needed. This can be an excellent opportunity to demonstrate a revision strategy or reinforce a convention you want students to employ in their own work.

- Now that you've created your very own informational mentor text, celebrate with your students!

Some of Our Favorite Well-Crafted Informational Books

Title, Author	Brief Summary
Ivan: The Remarkable True Story of the Shopping Mall Gorilla (Applegate, 2014)	The nonfiction companion book to *The One and Only Ivan*, this book tells the story of Ivan from his life at the shopping mall to the Atlanta Zoo.
A Little Book of Sloth (Cooke, 2013)	Information about sloths told from the perspective of sloths living in a sloth sanctuary in Costa Rica.
Some Bugs (DiTerlizzi, 2014)	A variety of bugs in an engaging text with colorful illustrations throughout the book.
The Cod's Tale (Kurlansky, 2014)	A story about the plentiful and well-known fish that populates the Atlantic Ocean. Includes scientific information about the cod and its habitat, but also its role in history.

Guided Practice and Independent Practice

Release responsibility to students as they create informational texts based on their research notes. Be prepared to check in with them often and provide support as needed. Final copies can take a variety of forms, from traditional research papers to informational pieces kept in the classroom or school library to serve as mentor texts!

Inquiry Experience: Study, Write, and Present on Historical People, Places, or Events

TARGETS

- I can define how informational text helps me learn about a historical person, place, or event.
- I can gather facts about my chosen topic.
- I can create a timeline, poster, or other visual to represent my thinking about my topic.

PREPARATION

- Choose a variety of mentor texts related to a historical period that you are studying. Include people, places, and events that you think will interest your students and build their background knowledge.
- Include as many primary sources as you can find. The Library of Congress has resources for teachers (www.loc.gov); in addition, some of our favorite texts for young historians are found below.
- Prepare an interactive whiteboard or chart paper to create a T-chart for students.

Informational Books for Budding Historians

Title, Author	Brief Summary
Rushmore (Curlee, 1999)	The story of the immigrant sculptor who created one of the largest, most famous sculptures in the country . . . Mt. Rushmore.
The Crossing (Napoli, 2011)	The story of the crossing of Lewis and Clark told from the perspective of Sacagawea's baby, whom Sacagawea carried on her back.
Nelson Mandela (Nelson, 2013)	The story of a young boy living in Africa who decides that he wants to grow up and make a difference. He eventually grows up to become president and fights for equality for all in South Africa.
John, Paul, George & Ben (Smith, 2006)	The story of the founding fathers told with a fresh "voice." These lads got into some trouble and took a few "liberties," which we Americans have benefited from all these years later.

EXPLANATION

The new standards expect that students in grades 3–5 should be able to gather information from sources and take notes on that information. Beginning in grade 4, students should be able to explain how authors use evidence to support their points in informational text. Encouraging students to consult a variety of informational texts for their research, including primary sources, broadens students' knowledge base and exposes them to a variety of ways to present information.

EXPERIENCE

Day 1—Choose topics.

Have students choose their topics based on your selected historical time period. It can be helpful to create a list of potential topics from which students can choose, including people, places, and events from the given time.

Day 2—Preview sources.

- Share available resources with students to preview once they have chosen their topics to research. If you have done the Conducting Research experience, remind students about the type of resources you explored then. (See page 143.)

- Introduce students to primary sources and explain their value in studying historical topics. Discuss the difference between a primary source—written by someone who experienced the event—and secondary sources, such as textbooks, articles, and informational books, which are written after the fact by people without firsthand knowledge of the time or event. (Be sure to have a variety of mentor text sources for students to explore and compare the differences.)

- Create a T-chart of the differences between primary and secondary sources on an interactive whiteboard or chart paper for student reference.

- Remember to read and discuss both the author's notes and back matter (found at the beginning and end of the book), which often include primary-source documents and other helpful information to guide young researchers.

Days 3–5—Research and gather information.

- Provide time for students to gather 10–15 facts about their selected topic.
- Provide a variety of resources, both text and multimedia, that will help students learn about their topics. They can also access primary sources either through texts or online.

Day 6—Evaluating research and sources.

- As students are wrapping up their research and getting ready to share their information, invite them to review their notes and the sources they used to gather their information.
- Which sources were most helpful in providing information for the topic?
- How did they utilize sources during the process as researchers to help them gather information?

Days 7–9—Creating a timeline, poster or other visual.

- As the culminating activity, students make a visual representation of information they've learned about their chosen topic. Go back to the mentor texts and the anchor chart, and see how the authors have creatively communicated information about their historical topics. Look closely at the text features that authors have used to communicate history in their writing. Encourage students to think about how they might use a visual to tell readers about their topic.
- Provide time for students to create a visual that incorporates their research about their topic.

Day 10—Polish and share.

Invite parents and/or other classes to your room to see how students have visually represented information on their topic—and become experts on it.

Big Idea: Craft Narratives

TRANSFORMING TEACHING	
Students write journal entries or stories.	Students engage in a variety of narrative writing experiences that vary in depth and length, including journals, personal narratives, stories, and so on.

Inquiry Experience: Craft a Personal Narrative

TARGET

I can write a narrative based on my personal experiences.

PREPARATION

- Gather a variety of personal narrative fiction books to share with students as mentor texts.
- Prepare chart paper to serve as an anchor chart.
- Decide where students will draft their personal narrative pieces. Some possibilities include:
    - ❋ Writer's notebook

* Writing spiral notebook (separate from writer's notebook)
* Notebook paper (Completed work may be kept in folder.)
* Word processing document

- Strategically pair students with a partner for revision/editing of completed pieces.

A Few Favorite Books That Tell Personal Stories

Title, Author	Brief Summary	
Year of the Jungle (Collins, 2013)	The story of Suzy and her family as they deal with her father's deployment to Vietnam. It tells about her struggles while he is gone and what life is like when he returns.	SUZANNE COLLINS YEAR OF THE JUNGLE — Illustrated by James Proimos
The Raft (LaMarche, 2000)	Nicky isn't thrilled about spending the summer in Wisconsin with his grandmother. When he gets there, his boredom turns into exploration when he finds a raft and begins to meets the wildlife nearby.	
My Rotten Redheaded Older Brother (Polacco, 1994)	Tricia can't stand her older brother because he does everything better than she can. One day she decides to change that and wishes on a shooting star that she can do something better than he can. When the carnival comes to town, she tries to ride the merry-go-round longer than him. Will she be successful?	
My Best Friend (Rodman, 2005)	It's summertime, and Lily is spending time at the pool. She wants to find a best friend. She tries to impress Tamika so that she will be her friend, but Tamika doesn't seem to want to be her friend. Lily doesn't understand why. Will she be able to find a best friend before the summer is over?	

EXPLANATION

In *The Writing Thief: Using Mentor Texts to Teach the Craft of Writing* (2014), Ruth Culham emphasizes the power of story and discusses how writers use narrative in both fiction and informational text to engage the reader. One of the best ways to get our students writing narratives is to help them find their own stories and develop them. Sharing a variety of mentor texts is a great starting point for helping young writers see that even small moments from their lives can make wonderful stories.

EXPERIENCE

Days 1–2—Read aloud and discuss mentor texts with a personal narrative focus.

- Collaboratively with students, identify characteristics of a well-written personal narrative and create an anchor chart to refer to during the writing process. (See an example on page 151.) Post the chart in your classroom and/or place copies in writer's notebooks.

- Encourage students to search their mentor texts for features of craft and structure, such as dialogue, flashbacks, or suspense. Invite students to incorporate these into their own writing.

Day 3—Select a topic.

- Think aloud as you discuss ideas for your own narrative piece and then choose a "small moment" (Fletcher & Portalupi, 2001), a snapshot from daily life, to write about. Invite students to go back into their writer's notebooks to select small moments of their own, or brainstorm together a list of possible topics, such as the first day of school, participating in a competition, making a new friend, visiting a new place, and so on.

- Review the anchor chart for the characteristics of well-written personal narratives.

Days 4–6—Write the body.

- Model writing the body of your personal narrative for students. We choose to begin with the body section because it focuses students on the heart of the piece.

- Think aloud as you write transitions and any special elements you want students to focus their attention on, such as dialogue or detailed description. Model pausing to reread what you've written before writing a new paragraph, and don't be afraid to cross out, rewrite, or otherwise mark up your draft.

- Provide time for students to write their body section.

- If they are writing on paper, have students write paragraphs on separate sheets or leave a space at the beginning of the piece so they can go back later and write the lead/introduction to their story.

- As students write, circulate and confer as needed.

Day 7—Revise with peer feedback.

- Pair students to give descriptive feedback on each other's writing. Tell students to focus on content only during this peer conference. (See Tips for Peer Feedback at right and in the online resources, page 160.) After receiving feedback, have them revise their writing.

Days 8–9—Write the introduction and conclusion.

- Model writing the introduction and conclusion to your own piece, thinking aloud as you make choices.

- After modeling each, have students write their own introduction and conclusion.

- Then have students confer with peers on the content of introductions and conclusions.

- After receiving feedback, have students revise their writing.

Days 10–12—Publish and confer.

- If you choose to have students publish, have them first do a final revision and edit using the checklists found in the online resources.

- Confer with writers on their pieces, give feedback, and set goals as needed.

Day 13 . . . and beyond—Share and celebrate.

- Share and celebrate students' pieces with classmates and others in the school community.

GOOD PERSONAL NARRATIVE WRITING CONTAINS THESE ELEMENTS:

- Real, important events from the writer's life

- A "small moment" in a writer's life

- A strong lead

- Descriptive, sensory details

- Usually told in first person

- Usually follow the "beginning, middle, and end" sequence

- A strong ending

Brainstorm with your students the characteristics of personal narrative writing.

Inquiry Experience: Write a Story

TARGETS

- I can understand the structure of a story.
- I can identify how story elements tell a story.
- I can create my own story using story elements.

PREPARATION

- Gather a variety of mentor texts that tell narrative fiction stories. Choose books that have clear, engaging story elements—character, setting, problem, and solution.
- Make class sets of the Writing Your Story With CLAPS organizer and the Writing Reflection Sheet (see online resources, page 160). Prepare an enlarged version of the CLAPS organizer to use for modeling.
- Prepare blank books for creating "little books;" see box on page 153.
- Strategically pair students with a partner for revision/editing after pieces are completed.

EXPLANATION

As students move from the primary grades to the intermediate grades, they may have fewer opportunities to write stories. As a result, these students often tend to ramble on and lack focus in their writing. The best way to help students write well-written narrative stories is to expose them to a variety of mentor texts that clearly demonstrate the basic elements of story structure.

Great Books for Learning About Story Elements

Title, Author	Brief Summary
Extra Yarn (Barnett, 2012)	Annabelle knits beautiful things for the people around her. One day a greedy king wants to steal her magic yarn. What will happen when he tries to take something that isn't his?
Clever Jack Takes the Cake (Fleming, 2010)	A poor boy named Jack is accidentally invited to the princess's birthday party. He bakes a cake, but it is eaten bit by bit on the way to the party. When he gets there, he amuses the princess with the story and ends up giving her the best gift of all!
This Is a Moose (Morris, 2014)	A director wants to capture the life of a moose on film, but the moose has other plans. The moose wants to be an astronaut and wants to share his dream on film! His friends want to help him, too. What's a frustrated film director to do?
Super Hair-O and the Barber of Doom (Rocco, 2013)	Super Hair-O gets his super powers from his shock of red hair on the top of his head. He and his friends all have that in common until the day that they are all dragged to the dreaded barber for haircuts. They anticipate that they will lose their superpowers forever!
Battle Bunny (Scieszka & Barnett, 2013)	Alex gets a sappy picture book for his birthday called "Birthday Bunny." He decides that through a little revision, he will make it more interesting and "Battle Bunny" is born!

Using CLAPS to Write Your Story

❋ **Character**—Who is your story about?

❋ **Location**—Where does your story take place?

❋ **Action**—What is your character doing at the beginning of the story?

❋ **Problem**—What is the problem your character faces?

❋ **Solution**—How does your character solve his/her problem?

(Fuhler & Walther, 2007)

Name:			Date:	
Writing Your Story With CLAPS				
Character(s)	Location(s)	Action(s)	Problem(s)	Solution(s)

EXPERIENCE

Days 1–6—Read aloud several of your selected mentor texts.

- Introduce students to the CLAPS chart above and discuss how it reflects the story elements found in books that you've been reading.

- Model filling in the CLAPS chart for a book or two, showing students how to identify the characteristics of fictional narrative writing in the mentor texts.

- Release responsibility to your students when they are ready by having them start to add other texts you've read, or books they've read independently, to the chart. Have students discuss the contents of these charts in collaborative conversations using the following questions:

  ❋ How do authors use elements in CLAPS to help them write a fictional narrative story?

  ❋ How might I use the CLAPS organizer to help me when I am writing a fictional narrative story?

Days 7–8—Plan stories.

- Invite students to brainstorm possible topics for their own fictional narrative story. Have them choose one from their list to develop into a story.

- Have them complete the CLAPS chart for their story idea.

- After completing their chart, have them get together with a partner and practice telling their story, remembering to include all the story elements on their CLAPS chart.

Tips for Making and Managing Little Books for Intermediate Writers

❋ Make an assortment of "little books" (blank or lined paper) in various sizes with varying number of pages.

  - 5½- x 8½-inch (½ sheet of copy paper portrait, staple some on top and some on side)

  - 4½- x 11-inch (½ sheet of copy paper landscape, staple some on top and some on side)

❋ Begin by giving students one book for the narrative that they written for the purpose of this inquiry experience or "assignment."

❋ Designate a place where students can go to get other little books if they would like to put other personal narrative or fiction stories that they have written in "little book" format to publish. (This is a great alternative to publishing student writing online or in other formats.)

❋ During writing workshop, create a plan with your writers to share little books with others in your classroom writing community or with their buddies in a younger grade. These are also great for assessment data or to share at a conference with parents.

(Adapted from Walther, 2015)

Day 9-12—*Draft, revise, and publish stories.*

- When students are ready to draft their stories, introduce them to "little books" (Walther, 2015). These books consist of blank half-sheets of paper stapled together, where students can write their stories and later include illustrations. Students may draft, revise, and edit in these books, or they may draft elsewhere and use these books for a final copy.

- During the writing process, have students complete the Writing Reflection Sheet (see online resources, page 160) to think about how they have grown as writers during the process.

- Once books are complete, have students share them together and with other readers in your school community!

Big Idea: Write Poetry

TRANSFORMING TEACHING

Poetry writing mainly occurs during an isolated unit and may only focus on one or two forms, like acrostics or rhyming poems.	Poetry writing is incorporated throughout the year, and students are encouraged to write different types of poems about a variety of topics of interest, including reading, math, science, and social studies.

Inquiry Experience: Write a Poem

TARGET

I can use what I have learned about poetry to write my own poems.

PREPARATION

- Gather a selection of poems and poetry collections to read aloud from.

- Prepare chart paper to collect students' observations about poetic elements.

- Make a class set of the Sensory Image Chart (see online resources, page 160). Prepare an enlarged copy for modeling.

- Provide 12–15 3- by 5-inch index cards per student, along with a plastic bag for storage for each student.

Some of Our Favorite Poetry Mentor Texts

Title, Author	Brief Summary
Falling Down the Page: A Book of List Poems (Heard, 2009)	A collection of poems about a variety of topics written in list form.
Firefly July (Janeczko, 2014)	Thirty-six short poems organized by season that are authored by various poets such as: Emily Dickinson, James Stevenson, Ralph Fletcher, and others.

Title, Author	Brief Summary
Doodle Dandies: Poems That Take Shape (Lewis, 1998)	Short poems whose forms take the shape of the topic of the poem (shape poems).
Hi, Koo! A Year of Seasons (Muth, 2014)	A seasonal collection of haiku poetry utilizing the reader's senses.
Lemonade and Other Poems Squeezed From a Single Word (Raczka, 2011)	Poems that start with a single word but then morph into a puzzle for the reader. This collection is enjoyable to read and ponder.

EXPLANATION

Poetry is often overlooked and underutilized as an instructional tool in our writing workshop. Regular exposure to poetry has value for students in big and small ways. In *Poetry Mentor Texts: Making Reading and Writing Connections, K–8* (2012), Lynne Dorfman and Rose Cappelli list these beneficial aspects:

- Poetry helps us better understand our experiences and ourselves.
- Poetry fits into all areas of the curriculum and bridges reading and writing workshop.
- Poetry encourages students to play with language and use words creatively to captivate the reader.
- Poetry can provide writers with a voice to communicate about events and experiences that may be difficult to enunciate through traditional writing.

EXPERIENCE

Days 1–3—Read aloud poetry.

- Immerse students in poetry by reading a variety of poetry on a daily basis.
- Encourage students to bring in their favorite poems to share and discuss.

Days 4-5—Chart poetic elements.

- During shared-writing time, notice and name the elements of engaging poems and create a class anchor chart. In addition to specific nouns, descriptive adjectives, and vivid verbs, students may also notice some of the elements in the chart on page 87. Remember to keep your anchor chart posted for students to reference and/or provide copies for them to paste in their writer's notebook.

Days 6–8—Choose topics and brainstorm sensory details.

- Demonstrate for your students how to go about creating a poem focusing on the senses and a single noun (Dorfman and Cappelli, 2012).

- Review for students the five senses. You can pass out a sensory chart like the one shown at right (available in online resources; see page 160) or have students record the senses in their writer's notebook.

- Invite students to brainstorm a list of topics that interest them or are related to a topic of study and then choose one to be the subject of a poem.

Sample Chart for "Snowflake"

Sight	Sound	Smell	Taste	Touch
white	silent	fresh and clean	sweet	cold
beautiful	whishing through the air	faint	wet	icy
glimmers in the moonlight	quiet as a mouse	brisk like winter	like candy	frigid

- Review with students what part of speech a noun is, then ask them to brainstorm nouns related to their topic.

- Ask students to choose a noun to be the focus of their poem. Model how to complete the senses chart—recording words or phrases that relate to the noun based on how the senses affect or are affected by the noun. Have students complete their own chart for their chosen noun.

Day 9—Share ideas with a partner.

- Have students work with a partner to share their charts. Encourage them to share their thinking and add to, or make changes to, the chart based on their conversations.

- Then have each student write each word or phrase on a 3- x 5-inch card and place the cards in a plastic bag.

Days 10–11—Write and revise poems.

- Each student takes out his or her cards and begins to arrange them into a poem. Students first work individually and then with a partner create a poem with their words.

- You may give each student extra blank index cards for words such as "a," "an," "the," etc., but no other "real" words are allowed.

- Encourage your poets to use only the words they have put on their cards and their original noun. (This is the challenge!)

- After they have created their poem, have partnerships share with other pairs, making small groups of four.

- Encourage each student to continue to rearrange and revise as many times as he or she would like. Remind them that's what real poets, and real writers, do—it's called revising!

Day 12—Share and celebrate!

- You can have your students copy their poems onto paper to put into a poetry binder to share with others, or continue to keep their cards in order to keep making new poems!

Looking Back, Moving Forward

Your professional expertise is the key when selecting from this menu of standards-focused learning experiences and integrating them across the days, weeks, and months of your already busy school year. One of the best ways to make these decisions is with a wise colleague by your side—that's what we do! These professional conversations will deepen your understanding of the standards, and the reflections you share after trying out an experience will strengthen your teaching. To guide you in your planning, the online resources (see page 160) include a variety of templates and tools that should help you organize your instruction.

Professional Resources Cited

Allington, R. (2013). What really matters when working with struggling readers. *The Reading Teacher, 66*(7), 520-530.

Allington, R. & Johnston, P. (Eds.). (2002). *Reading to learn: Lessons from exemplary fourth-grade classrooms.* New York: Guilford.

Anderson, J. (2005). *Mechanically inclined: Building grammar, usage, and style into writer's workshop.* Portland, ME: Stenhouse Publishers.

Atwell, N. (2007). *The reading zone: How to help kids become skilled, passionate, habitual, critical readers.* New York: Scholastic.

Beck, I., McKeown, M., & Kucan, L. (2013). *Bringing words to life: Robust vocabulary instruction.* New York: Guilford.

Bennett, S. (2007). *That workshop book: New systems and structures for classrooms that read, write, and think.* Portsmouth, NH: Heinemann.

Calkins, L., Ehrenworth, M., & Lehman, C. (2012). *Pathways to the common core: Accelerating achievement.* Portsmouth, NH: Heinemann.

Chappuis, J. (2009). *Seven strategies of assessment for learning.* Boston, MA: Pearson.

Coleman, D. & Pimental, S. (2012). *Revised publishers' criteria for the Common Core State Standards in English language arts and literacy, grades 3–12.* Washington, DC: Council of Chief State School Officers.

Culham, R. (2014). *The writing thief: Using mentor texts to teach the craft of writing.* Newark, DE: International Reading Association.

Dorfman, L. & Capelli, R. (2012). *Poetry mentor texts: Making reading and writing connections: K–8.* Portland, ME: Stenhouse Publishers.

Fisher, D. & Frey, N. (2012). Close reading in elementary schools. *The Reading Teacher, 66*(3), 179-188.

Fletcher, R. (1996). *A writer's notebook: Unlocking the writer within you.* New York: Avon Books.

Fletcher, R. & Portalupi, J. (2001). *Writing workshop: The essential guide.* Portsmouth, NH: Heinemann.

Fuhler, C. & Walther, M. (2010). *Teaching struggling readers with poetry: Engaging poems with mini-lessons that target and teach phonics, sight words, fluency, and more, laying the foundation for reading success.* New York: Scholastic.

Fuhler, C. & Walther, M. (2007). *Literature is back!: Using the best books for teaching readers and writers across genres.* New York: Scholastic.

Gallagher, K. (2011). *Write like this: Teaching real-world writing through modeling & mentor texts.* Portland, ME: Stenhouse Publishers.

Graves, D. (1983). *Writing: Teachers and children at work.* Portsmouth, NH: Heinemann.

Graves, D. (1994). *A fresh look at writing.* Portsmouth, NH: Heinemann.

Harvey, S. & Daniels, H. (2009). *Comprehension and collaboration: Inquiry circles in action.* Portsmouth, NH: Heinemann.

Hiebert, E. & Pearson, D. (2013). What happens to the basics? *Educational Leadership, 70*(4), 48–36.

International Reading Association Common Core State Standards (CCSS) Committee. (2012). Literacy implementation guidance for the ELA Common Core State Standards [White paper]. Retrieved from http://www.reading.org/Libraries/association-documents/ira_ccss_guidelines.pdf

Johnston, P. (2004). *Choice words: How our language affects children's learning.* Portland, ME: Stenhouse.

Johnston, P. (2012). *Opening minds: Using language to change lives.* Portland: ME: Stenhouse.

Keene, E. O. (2012). *Talk about understanding: Rethinking classroom talk to enhance comprehension.* Portsmouth, NH: Heinemann.

Krashen, S. (2004). *The power of reading: Insights from the research.* Portsmouth, NH: Heinemann.

Lehman, C. & Roberts, K. (2013). *Falling in love with close reading: Lessons for analyzing texts and life.* Portsmouth, NH: Heinemann.

Lehman, C. (2012). *Energize research reading and writing: Fresh strategies to spark interest, develop independence, and meet key common core standards.* Portsmouth, NH: Heinemann.

Macon, J., Bewell, D., & Vogt, M. E. (1991). *Responses to literature.* Newark, DE: International Reading Association.

Miller, D. (2013). I can create mental images to retell and infer big ideas. *The Reading Teacher, 66*(5), 360-364.

Miller, D. & Kelley, S. (2013). *Reading in the wild: The book whisperer's keys to cultivating lifelong reading habits.* San Francisco, CA: Jossey-Bass.

Miller, D. & Moss, B. (2013). *No more independent reading without support.* Portsmouth, NH: Heinemann.

National Governors Association Center for Best Practices (NGA Center) and Council of Chief State School Officers (CCSSO) (2010). Common core state standards initiative. Washington, D.C.: Authors. (www.corestandards.org)

National Commission on Writing. (2003, April). The neglected r: The need for a writing revolution. Available at www.collegeboard.com

NGSS Lead States. (2013). *Next generation science standards: For states, by states.* Washington, DC: The National Academies Press.

Nichols, M. (2006). *Comprehension through conversation: The power of purposeful talk in the reading workshop.* Portsmouth, NH: Heinemann.

Overturf, B. J., Montgomery, L. H., & Smith, M. H. (2013). *Word nerds: Teaching all students to learn and love vocabulary.* Portland, ME: Stenhouse Publishers.

Pearson, P. D. (2011). Toward the next generation of comprehension instruction: A coda. In Daniels, H. (Eds.). *Comprehension going forward where we are/what's next.* (pp. 243–253). Portsmouth, NH: Heinemann.

Pearson, P. D. & Gallagher, M.C. (1983). The instruction of reading comprehension. *Contemporary Educational Psychology, 8,* 317–344.

Rasinski, T. (2012). Why reading fluency should be hot! *The Reading Teacher, 65*(8), 516-522.

Richardson, J. & Walther, M. (2013). *Next step guided reading assessment 3–6.* New York: Scholastic.

Roskos, K. & Neuman, S. (2012). Formative assessment: Simply, no additives. *The Reading Teacher 65*(8), 534–538.

Routman, R. (2004). *Writing essential: Raising expectations and results while simplifying teaching.* Portsmouth, NH: Heinemann.

Routman, R. (2008). *Teaching essentials: Expecting the most and getting the best from every learner, K–8.* Portsmouth, NH: Heinemann.

Stuhlman, M. W., & Pianta, R. C. (2009). Profiles of educational quality in first grade. *Elementary School Journal, 109*(4), 323–342. doi:10.1086/593936

Vygotsky, L. (1962). *Thought and language.* Cambridge, MA: MIT Press.

Walther, M. (2015). *Transforming literacy teaching in the era of higher standards: K–2.* New York: Scholastic.

Walther, M. & Phillips, K. (2009). *Month-by-month trait-based writing instruction: ready-to-use lessons and strategies for weaving morning messages, read-alouds, and more into your daily writing program.* New York: Scholastic.

Walther, M. & Phillips, K. (2012). *Month-by-month reading instruction for the differentiated classroom.* New York: Scholastic.

Wilde, S. (2014). *Quantity and quality: Increasing the volume and complexity of students' reading.* Portsmouth, NH: Heinemann.

Children's Literature Cited

Adoff, A. (2000). *Touch the poem.* New York: Blue Sky Press.

Angleberger, T. (2010). *The strange case of Origami Yoda.* New York: Amulet Books.

Applegate, K. (2014). *Ivan: The remarkable true story of the shopping mall gorilla.* New York: Clarion Books.

Auch, M. & Auch, H. (2009). *The plot chickens.* New York: Holiday House.

Banks, K. (2013). *City cat.* New York: Frances Foster.

Barnett, M. (2012). *Extra yarn.* New York: Balzer & Bray.

Barnett, M. (2014). *Sam and Dave dig a hole.* Somerville, MA: Candlewick Press.

Barnett, M. (2014). *Telephone.* San Francisco: Chronicle Books.

Beaty, A. (2007). *Iggy Peck, architect.* New York: Abrams Books for Young Readers.

Beaty, A. (2013). *Rosie Revere, engineer.* New York: Abrams Books for Young Readers.

Becker, A. (2013). *Journey.* Somerville, MA: Candlewick Press.

Berne, J. (2013). *On a beam of light: A story of Albert Einstein.* San Francisco, CA: Chronicle.

Bloom, B. (1999). *Wolf!* New York: Orchard Books.

Bober, N. (2013). *Papa is a poet: A story about Robert Frost.* New York: Christy Ottaviano Books.

Bragg, G. (2014). *How they choked: Failures, flops, and flaws of the awfully famous.* New York: Walker Books for Young Readers.

Brennan-Nelson, D. (2004). *My teacher likes to say.* Ann Arbor, MI: Sleeping Bear Press.

Briggs, R. (1978). *The snowman.* New York: Random House.

Brown, J. (2013). *Star wars: Jedi academy.* New York: Scholastic.

Brown, P. (2013). *Mr. Tiger goes wild.* New York: Little, Brown.

Bruno, E. (2009). *Punctuation celebration.* New York: Henry Holt.

Bunting, E. (2000). *The memory string.* New York: Clarion Books.

Buyea, R. (2010). *Because of Mr. Terupt.* New York: Delacorte Press.

Buzzeo, T. (2012). *One cool friend.* New York: Dial Books for Young Readers.

Carle, E. (2014). *What's your favorite animal?* New York: Henry Holt.

Cassino, M. (2009). *The story of snow: The science of winter's wonder.* San Francisco, CA: Chronicle Books.

Cavanaugh, N. (2013). *This journal belongs to Ratchet.* Naperville, Illinois: Sourcebooks Jabberwocky.

Chin, J. (2014). *Gravity.* New York: Roaring Book Press.

Christiansen, C. (1997). *The mitten tree.* New York: Scholastic.

Chung, A. (2014). *Ninja!* New York: Henry Holt.

Cleary, B. (2013). *Pre- and re-, mis- and dis-: What is a prefix?* Minneapolis, MN: Millbrook.

Cleary, B. (2014). *–ful and –less, -er and –ness: What is a suffix?* Minneapolis, MN: Millbrook.

Coffelt, N. (2012). *Aunt Ant leaves through the leaves: A story with homophones and homonyms.* New York: Scholastic.

Collins, S. (2013). *Year of the jungle.* New York: Scholastic.

Cooke, L. (2013). *A little book of sloth.* New York: Margaret K. McElderry Books.

Curlee, L. (1999). *Rushmore.* New York: Scholastic.

Dakos, K. (1996). *The goof who invented homework and other school poems.* New York: Dial Books.

Daly, C. (2014). *Emily's blue period.* New York: Roaring Brook Press.

Daywalt, D. (2013). *The day the crayons quit.* New York: Philomel.

DeGross, M. (1994). *Donavan's word jar.* New York: Harper Trophy.

DiPucchio, K. (2014). *Dog days of school.* New York: Disney-Hyperion.

DiTerlizzi, A. (2013). *Some bugs.* New York: Beach Lane Books.

Doltich, R. K. (2001). *When riddles come rumbling in.* Honesdale, PA: Wordsong.

Edwards, P. (2009). *The bus ride that changed history: The story of Rosa Parks.* New York: HMH Books for Young Readers.

Fanelli, S. (1995). *My map book.* New York: Harper Collins.

Fine, E. (2004). *Cryptomania! Teleporting into Greek and Latin with the Cryptokids.* Berkeley, CA: Tricycle.

Fleischman, P. (2013). *The matchbox diary.* Somerville, MA: Candlewick Press.

Fleming, C. (2010). *Clever Jack takes the cake.* New York: Schwartz & Wade Books.

Floca, B. (2009). *Moonshot: The flight of Apollo 11.* New York: Atheneum Books for Young Readers.

Floca, B. (2013). *Locomotive.* New York: Atheneum.

Fogliano, J. (2006). *And then it's spring.* New York: Roaring Brook Press.

Frazee, M. (2003). *Roller coaster.* San Diego: Harcourt.

Freedman, D. (2013). *The story of fish & snail.* New York: Viking Books.

Giovanni, N. (2007). *Rosa.* New York: Square Fish.

Grabenstein, C. (2013). *Escape from Mr. Lemoncello's library.* New York: Random House.

Graff, L. (2013). *A tangle of knots.* New York: Philomel Books.

Graff, L. (2014). *Absolutely almost.* New York: Philomel Books.

Grey, M. (2014). *Hermelin: The detective mouse.* New York: Knopf Books for Young Readers.

Hanlon, A. (2012). *Ralph tells a story.* Las Vegas, NV: Amazon Children's Books.

Heard, G. (Ed.) (2009). *Falling down the page.* New York: Roaring Brooks Press.

Heiligman, D. (2013). *The boy who loved math: The improbable life of Paul Erdös.* New York: Scholastic.

Henkes, K. (2013). *The year of Billy Miller.* New York: Greenwillow Books.

Holm, J. (2007). *Middle school is worse than meatloaf.* New York: Atheneum Books for Young Readers.

Holub, J. (2013). *Little red writing.* San Francisco, CA: Chronicle Books.

Idle, M. (2013). *Flora and the flamingo.* San Francisco, CA: Chronicle Books.

Isabella, J. (2013). *Chitchat: Celebrating the world's language.* Toronto, ON: Kids Can Press.

Janeczko, P. (2014). *Firefly July: A year of very short poems.* Somerville, MA: Candlewick Press.

Jeffers, O. (2008). *The great paper chase.* New York: Harper Collins.

Joyce, W. (2012). *The fantastic flying books of Mr. Morris Lessmore.* New York: Atheneum Books for Young Readers.

Kalman, M. (2012). *Looking at Lincoln.* New York: Nancy Paulsen Books.

Kavanaugh, N. (2012). *This journal belongs to Ratchet.* Naperville, IL: Sourcebooks.

Klausmeier, J. (2013). *Open this little book.* San Francisco, CA: Chronicle Books.

Klassen, J. (2011). *I want my hat back.* Somerville, MA: Candlewick Press.

Klassen, J. (2012). *This is not my hat.* Somerville, MA: Candlewick Press.

Klise, K. (2010). *Stand straight, Ella Kate.* New York: Dial Books for Young Readers.

Korman, G. (2012). *Ungifted.* New York: Balzer & Bray.

Kostecki-Shaw, J. (2011). *Same, same but different.* New York: Christy Ottaviano Books.

Krosoczka, J. (2014). *Peanut Butter and Jellyfish.* New York: Alfred A. Knopf.

Kurlansky, M. (2001). *The cod's tale.* New York: Putnam's.

Kurlansky, M. (2006). *The story of salt.* New York: G. P. Putnam's Sons.

LaMarche, J. (2000). *The raft.* New York: Harper Collins.

Laminack, L. (2004). *Saturdays and teacakes.* Atlanta, GA: Peachtree.

LaRochelle, D. (2004). *The best pet of all.* New York: Dutton Children's.

Leedy, L. (2008). *Crazy like a fox: A simile story.* New York: Holiday House.

Levine, E. (2007). *Henry's freedom box: A true story of the Underground Railroad.* New York: Scholastic.

Lewis, J. (1998). *Doodle dandies: Poems that take shape.* New York: Atheneum Books for Young Readers.

Lewis, J. (2012). *Edgar Allan Poe's pie: Math puzzlers in classic poems.* New York: Scholastic.

Lichtenheld, T. (2010). *Bridget's beret.* New York: Christy Ottaviano.

Lloyd, N. (2014). *A snicker of magic.* New York: Scholastic.

Loewen, N. (2011). *You're toast and other metaphors we adore.* North Mankato, MN: Picture Window.

Ludwig, T. (2013). *The invisible boy.* New York: Alfred A. Knopf.

Lyon, G. (1999). *Book.* New York: DK Children.

Lyon, G. (2011). *All the water in the world.* New York: Atheneum.

McReynolds, L. (2012). *Eight days gone.* Watertown, MA: Charlesbridge.

MacLachlan, P. (1995). *What you know first.* New York: Joanna Cutler.

MacLachlan, P. (2010). *Word after word after word.* New York: Katherine Tegen Books.

Madormo, J. (2012). *The homemade stuffing caper: Book 1.* New York: Philomel Books.

Manna, A. & Mitakidou, S. (2011). *The orphan: A Cinderella story from Greece.* New York: Schwartz & Wade Books.

Martin, Jr., B. (2008). *The Bill Martin Jr big book of poetry.* New York: Simon & Schuster.

Martin, R. (1992). *The rough-face girl.* New York: Puffin Books.

Mass, W. (2010). *11 birthdays.* New York: Scholastic.

Mass, W. (2010). *The candymakers.* New York: Little, Brown.

McDonnell, P. (2011). *Me. . . Jane.* New York: Little, Brown.

Meltzer, B. (2014). *I am Rosa Parks.* New York: Dial Books for Young Readers.

Morris, R. (2014). *This is a moose.* New York; Boston: Little, Brown and Company.

Moss, M. (2006). *Amelia's notebook.* New York: Simon & Schuster Books for Young Readers.

Munson, D. (2000). *Enemy pie.* San Francisco, CA: Chronicle Books.

Muth, J. (2014). *Hi, Koo! A year of seasons.* New York: Scholastic.

Napoli, D. (2011). *The crossing.* New York: Atheneum Books for Young Readers.

Nelson, K. (2013). *Nelson Mandela.* New York: Katherine Tegen Books.

Offill, J. (2014). *Sparky!* New York: Schwartz & Wade Books.

Otoshi, K. (2008). *One.* San Rafael, CA: KO Kids.

Otoshi, K. (2014). *Two.* San Rafael, CA: KO Kids Books.

Parish, P. (2013). *Amelia Bedelia.* New York: Greenwillow Books.

Pastis, S. (2013). *Timmy Failure: Mistakes were made.* Somerville, MA: Candlewick Press.

Pett, M. (2011). *The girl who made mistakes.* Naperville, IL: Sourcebooks Jabberwocky.

Pett, M. (2014). *The girl and the bicycle.* New York: Simon & Schuster.

Palacio, R. J. (2012). *Wonder.* New York: Knopf Books for Young Readers.

Polacco, P. (1994). *My rotten redheaded older brother.* New York: Simon & Schuster Books for Young Readers.

Polacco, P. (1998). *Thank you, Mr. Falker.* New York: Philomel.

Polacco, P. (2011). *Bun bun button.* New York: G. P. Putnam's Sons.

Polacco, P. (2011). *Just in time, Abraham Lincoln.* New York: G. P. Putnam's Sons.

Polacco, P. (2014). *Clara and Davie: The true story of Clara Barton.* New York: Scholastic.

Portis, A. (2014). *Froodle.* New York: Roaring Brook Press.

Prelutsky, J. (1990). *Something big has been here.* New York: Greenwillow Books.

Prelutsky, J. (2012). *I've lost my hippopotamus.* New York: Greenwillow Books.

Pulver. R. (2011). *Happy endings: A story about suffixes.* New York: Scholastic.

Raczka, B. (2011). *Lemonade and other poems squeezed from a single word.* New York: Square Fish.

Rappaport, D. (2010). *Jack's path of courage: The life of John F. Kennedy.* New York: Disney-Hyperion Books.

Ray, M. (2011). *Stars.* New York: Beach Lane Books.

Reynolds, A. (2013). *Carnivores.* New York: San Francisco, CA: Chronicle Books.

Reynolds, P. (2004). *Ish.* Boston, MA: Walker.

Reynolds, P. & Reynolds, P. (2014). *Going places.* New York: Atheneum Books.

Rickerty, S. (2014). *The crayon: A colorful tale about friendship.* New York: Aladdin.

Ringgold, F. (1999). *If a bus could talk.* New York: Simon & Schuster Books for Young People.

Roberts, J. (2014). *The smallest girl in the smallest grade.* New York: G. P. Putnam's Sons.

Robinson, S. (2014). *Under the same sun.* New York: Scholastic.

Rocco, J. (2013). *Super Hair-O and the barber of doom.* New York: Disney*Hyperion Books.

Rodman, M. (2005). *My best friend.* New York: Viking.

Ruddell, D. (2007). *Today at the Bluebird Café.* New York: Margaret K. McElderry Books.

Russell, R. (2009). *The dork diaries: Tales from a not so fabulous life.* New York: Aladdin.

Schaefer, L. (2013). *Lifetime: The amazing numbers in animal lives.* San Francisco, CA: Chronicle Books.

Schotter, R. (2006). *The boy who loved words.* New York: Schwartz & Wade Books.

Scieszka, J. & Barnett, M. (2013). *Battle bunny.* New York: Simon & Schuster.

Seuss, Dr. (1971). *The lorax.* New York, Random House.

Sidman, J. (2011). *Swirl by swirl: Spirals in nature.* New York: Houghton Mifflin.

Simon, S. (2006). *Stars.* New York: HarperCollins.

Simon, S. (2009). *Wolves.* New York: HarperCollins.

Singer, M. (2013). *Rutherford B., who was he? Poems about our presidents.* New York: Disney-Hyperion.

Smith, D. (2014). *If: A mind-bending new way of looking at big ideas and numbers.* Toronto: Kids Can Press.

Smith, L. (2006). *John, Paul, George & Ben.* New York: Hyperion Books.

Snicket, L. (2013). *The dark.* New York: Little, Brown.

Solheim, J. (2010). *Born yesterday.* New York: Philomel Books.

Spires, A. (2014). *The most magnificent thing.* Manitoba, CN: Kids Can Press.

Staake, B. (2013). *Bluebird.* New York: Random House.

Staake, B. (2014). *My pet book.* New York: Random House.

Steig, W. (2002). *Which would you rather be?* New York: Joanna Cotler.

Stevens, J. (2011). *Little red pen.* Boston: Harcourt Children's Books.

Stevenson, J. (1998). *Popcorn.* New York: Scholastic.

Tashjian, J. (2010). *My life as a book.* New York: Henry Holt.

Terban, M. (1983). *In a pickle and other funny idioms.* New York: Clarion Books.

Terban, M. (1993). *It figures! Fun figures of speech.* New York: Clarion Books.

Timberlake, A. (2013). *One came home.* New York: Alfred A. Knopf.

Tobin, J. (2013). *The very inappropriate word.* New York: Christy Ottaviano Books.

Walker, S. (2012). *Freedom song: The story of Henry "Box" Brown.* New York: Harper.

Williams, L. (2010). *The can man.* New York: Lee & Low.

Winter, J. (2013). *JFK.* New York: Katherine Tegen Books.

Woodson, J. (2012). *Each kindness.* New York: Nancy Paulsen Books.

Woodson, J. (2013). *This is the rope: A story from the Great Migration.* New York: Nancy Paulsen.

Young, C. (2011). *Ten birds.* Toronto, CN: Kids Can Press.

Online Resources

Go to teacherexpress.scholastic.com/transforming-literacy-teaching-3-5 to download or view the following free resources.

Downloadable Print Resources

- Reading Strategy Toolbox
- Status of the Class
- Books I've Read
- Someday List
- Editor's Checklist
- Writing Record Sheet
- Goal-Setting Form
- Prefix/Suffix Sheet
- Ladder of Text Complexity
- Making Inferences When I Read
- Characters' Response to Events
- Discovering Relationships Between Informational Texts
- Context Clues
- Annotating Texts
- Tips for Giving Peer Feedback
- Writing Reflection Sheet
- Writing Poetry: Sensory Image Chart
- Writing Your Story With CLAPS

Video Resources

- Classroom Tour
- Standards Integration in Action
- Reading Workshop in Action
- Writing Workshop in Action
- Teaching Routines in Action
- Inquiry Experiences—Reading in Action
- Inquiry Experiences—Writing in Action